GRANDMA'S GONE TO AFRICA

One Woman's Journey to Botswana the Good

Edelgard Mahant

EP2M Enterprises Inc.
Toronto, Canada

Photograph on page 98 reproduced with the permission of Mr. Etsogile Syntax Masoba.

All photos in this book (and some more) may be viewed in colour at https://www.facebook.com/Grandmasgonetoafrica

Quotation from Unity Dow, *The Screaming of the Innocent*, Melbourne: Spinifex Press, 2002, page 80, reproduced with the permission of Spinifex Press.

Cover design by Karin Jurgens.

Copyright © 2016 Edelgard Mahant

ISBN-13: 978-1522700128
ISBN-10: 1522700129

Table of Contents

Foreword iv

Acknowledgements vi

Glossary: People and Terms vii

Section A — Just the Bare Necessities

    Chapter 1   The Roofs Over My Head and the Yard Beneath My Feet 1

    Chapter 2   Food and Drink 39

    Interchapter   Little Pleasures of Life in Gaborone 69

    Chapter 3   Getting from A to B (and Back) 71

Section B — Friends, People, Society

    Chapter 4   Man, Woman, Sex 95

    Chapter 5   Weddings, Funerals, Churches 121

    Chapter 6   Crime — and Punishment? 137

    Chapter 7   All Around Botswana 153

    Chapter 8   University Life 175

An Introduction to Botswana — If You Want to Know More 195

Photos in full colour
https://www.facebook.com/Grandmasgonetoafrica

v

Foreword

What does a 67-year-old university professor do when she is deprived of the job she loves only because of an outdated and illogical rule called mandatory retirement? With the help of the internet, she finds the same kind of job in a more enlightened place where retirement is a matter of choice. In my case, that place was the wonderful African country of Botswana.

So in September 2008, I packed my bags, said good-bye to family and friends and set out for Botswana, a country in southern Africa, just north of the Republic of South Africa. That summer of 2008, the weather was beautiful in Toronto, and in our part of the city, known for its Greek heritage, the local business association was providing lovely, evocative Greek music twice a week. We would walk to the little open square on the corner, with its fake Greek temple and statue of Alexander the Great, and watch as people gathered to dance, singly or in groups. It was a magical scene, and I was going to leave all that behind to go to a strange place of which I knew little? I had never set foot in Africa south of the Sahara; indeed, except for a week-long holiday in Tunisia in 1973, I had never set foot on the continent. What I knew of Africa was probably not so different from what most Canadians know: starving women and children in refugee camps, child soldiers, torture and mutilation, civil war, and at the positive end of the spectrum, luxurious safari holidays.

I had done just a bit of background research. I bought a travel book on southern Africa. I spoke to an acquaintance who was in Botswana as a US Peace Corps volunteer. I looked at the country summary on the US State Department website and tried to determine what health measures the Canadian government recommended. The travel book was not much use; it made the country sound like a big safari experience. The Peace Corps girl assured me that life was pleasant and safe and that I should not hesitate to come. The *CIA World Factbook* told me that Botswana was a large, semi-arid country with a population of less than two million; indeed its population density was lower than that of Canada. The State Department site said that Botswana was a democracy, but had problems such as a high incidence of HIV/AIDS. The Canadian government site was not of much use either; it lumped Botswana together with other African countries.

The University of Botswana offered me a two-year contract and I told myself that no matter what, I would tough it out for at least one year. It took only two or three weeks for that resolution to become another one: if only I could stay longer, if only I could be a Canadian and enjoy Canadian life without giving up Botswana.

This is not a travel book, much less a book of advice for travellers. It is a book about life in another country, a country very different but yet not so different from Canada, the US or Europe. I believe that people all over the world, whatever, their race, background or religion, have much in common. It is the challenges that they face from day to day that differ.

Some of you may have the opportunity and the wish to travel; others may decide to stay at home. I do hope that after you have read this book, each one of you will wish that you could travel to Botswana, to a country whose people are polite and considerate and unbelievably welcoming to strangers, well most strangers, Zimbabweans excepted.

It is my fervent hope that after you have read this book, you will have a feel for what it is like to live in a country that is both modern and traditional, a country whose people aspire to modernity, which they sometimes achieve and sometimes fail to achieve in ways that are sad as well as funny and that your faith in humanity and in the similarity and the goodness of most of us will be strengthened and grow.

Edelgard Mahant
Toronto, Canada
February 2016

Acknowledgements

This book would not have been possible without the help of many good friends.

First and foremost, there is Dr. Xavier de Vanssay who gave me continuing support throughout from the drafting of the first chapter to the final formatting of the entire manuscript. And Grace Hyam who gave so much of her time reading and commenting on draft after draft.

Vivienne Monty, Mohan and Susan Grewal, Catherine Ukas and Elaine Porter all took the time to read the entire manuscript, and I am very grateful for the time they spent doing so and for the many helpful comments they made.

Tom Holzinger, Daniel Bodistean, Nicole Lebon, and Karin Jurgens provided useful assistance with preparing the manuscript for publication. Their expertise was invaluable.

My husband Parkash and son Paul tolerated my absence with varying amounts of goodwill and enjoyed their visits to Botswana. Our grandsons, John and William, did not have the opportunity to visit Africa because of the misconceptions that I hope this book will help to dispel.

In Botswana, several of my good friends took time to read portions of the manuscript and to provide me with useful information and feedback. In alphabetical order, they are Dr. Keb Lotshwao, Dr. Z. Maundeni, Dr. Basathu Mbongwe, Dr. Baakile Motshegwa, and Dr. Keletso Setlhabi.

And finally but not least, there are the many good friends in Botswana whose kindness, generosity, and willingness to accept me as one of their own has done so much to strengthen my belief in the common humanity of us all.

Although I am grateful for the help and advice of my friends, any remaining mistakes or opinions expressed are my responsibility.

E.M.

Glossary of People and Things

Batswana – the Setswana word for the people of Botswana

BDF – Botswana Defence Force

BTV – Botswana Television, a government-owned monopoly

Choppies – local discount supermarket chain

combi – a minibus used as public transit in southern Africa

Jason – the middle child of Syntax's and Sarah's three children

modisa – a person who looks after animals, a herdsman or shepherd

Motswana – the singular of Batswana

Parkash – my husband

papa – cornmeal porridge, a traditional staple

phapatha – a large baking powder biscuit, usually eaten for breakfast

Paul – my son

PEPFAR – the President of the United States' Emergency Plan for AIDS Relief

Pula (abbreviated P) – the Botswana currency, worth about 8 to one Canadian dollar in 2015; at the time of my stay there it was about 7 to the dollar; one pula equals 100 thebe

Riverwalk – a prominent mall in Gaborone, a magnet for foreigners

rondavel – the traditional house of southern Africa, with a circular wall of brick, stones, or earth, and a thatched roof of grass or straw

russian – a kind of large wiener sausage

samp – a porridge made of cracked corn, often served with beans

Sarah – Syntax's wife

seswaa – a meat dish of cooked beef that has been pounded and finely shredded, served on ceremonial occasions

Syntax – my regular, self-employed driver who became a good friend

UB – the University of Botswana

x

Chapter 1 The Roofs Over My Head (and the Yard beneath my Feet)

That day in September 2008 when I first arrived in Botswana, the chair of the department and the university housing manager met me at the airport. They brought me to Binnis, a bed-and-breakfast establishment that was literally kitty-corner from the university campus.

Binnis was a new guest house, gleaming clean with lots of white marble and large artificial flowers in the lobby. The rooms were basic, but they had most of the essentials: a bathroom with a shower or a bathtub, air conditioning and a television without cable which on different days produced different South African channels, as well as BTV (Botswana Television), which hardly anyone watched because it was for the most part dead boring. For university professors, the rooms at Binnis had one major disadvantage. There were no desks or tables. And there was no internet. (When I returned for a visit, in 2015, there were still no tables in the rooms, but there was high-speed internet.)

Binnis was small. It had only eight rooms. The four at the back had private facilities, and that is where all of us professors stayed. At the front there were four rooms that shared two bathrooms. This is where local people stayed, like the businessman and a female student who spent the night there together from time to time. The breakfast at Binnis was copious: a bowl of cornflakes, followed by two pieces of bread (public demand eventually produced brown bread), plenty of margarine to spread on that bread, a fried egg and one of those big wieners that are called russians in Botswana. To drink there was cold water, and there was hot water into which we could dip a tea bag or which we could mix with a cheap local brand of instant coffee. Sometimes there were also fresh fruits, such as oranges. Not a gourmet breakfast, but more than enough to see one through till lunchtime.

Those of us used to eating toast in the morning found the large slices of soft bread a bit hard to swallow. Eventually, one of us, a medical professor from Belfast, went to Game City (a store that was before long taken over by Walmart) and bought a toaster, which we plugged in on the sideboard, so that whoever wished could toast his or her bread. When the medical professor left and moved into a furnished apartment, he gave the toaster to me, and when I moved into my house, I took it with me. When I left, four years later, I gave it away. I didn't think that I should sell something I had not bought.

Before long, I contributed a jar of jam to our breakfasts. A theology professor from Ghana went to a conference in Finland and bought a large jar of blueberry jam, but we never got to taste it. Security at Helsinki airport took it from him. Who knew what could have been in that large jar labelled blueberry jam?

One of the best things about Binnis was the two young ladies who made and served us breakfast and kept the place sparkling clean. They were so friendly and helpful and always smiling. They called me Mma, and the couple from Northern Ireland Mom and Dad. For some extra money, they washed my laundry, which was always dry and ready on the same day. These young girls worked from six in the morning until mid-afternoon. Each of them had just one day a week off, and on that day the other managed to do all the work.

At night time there was one staff person only, a security guard who doubled as a receptionist. There was an outside gate that was locked after dark; a small parking lot separated the gate from the front door. The guard was outside in the yard most of the time but would go in if someone needed help. If something went wrong, such as a leaking water tap or a television that would not work, he would phone the manager. For most of the time that I stayed at Binnis, the guard was a young man called Andrew. He would invariably hit us up for money each time we walked by. He had a different story each time. For example, one time he said he needed money to pay the fee so that he could take his motorcycle license test. A couple of years later, when I was walking home from the supermarket to my house in the dark, someone called me from the combi stop. It was Andrew, and he wanted me to give him money! (Combis are the rundown minibuses that provide public transport throughout the urbanized parts of Botswana. See Chapter 3).

Getting to know professors who had arrived from other countries was another pleasant aspect of staying at Binnis. There was the couple from Northern Ireland. Harold was a professor of public medicine who was helping to set up the Faculty of Health Sciences. Harold was a bit shy, but his wife Marion was really pleasant. They rented a car almost as soon as they got there because they could not stand eating at the News Café (the only restaurant within walking distance) with its constant background noise of African music. They sometimes took me out to eat, giving my diet a bit of variety. A couple of times they invited me to functions in the evening which I could not have attended otherwise, such as a gospel concert and an evening which was supposed to feature the culture of different parts of Africa, but which turned out to be one long commercial for Western Union.

According to the United Nations, Botswana is a semi-arid country. It only rains between October and April, and then only occasionally, but for some strange reason or more likely no reason, it nearly always rained when Harold, Marion and I went out for the evening. That was a problem because in a tropical country many events are held outside. Marion began to call me a rainmaker. Perhaps I was, because one evening when the French embassy sponsored an event to celebrate something or other to do with the European Union in the yard of the National Museum, I invited a student who would be spending the next term on exchange in the Netherlands to come with me, so as to provide him with some acculturation. That night it rained and rained. The catering staff managed to carry the table with the hors d'oeuvres to a dry place, ditto for the wine table, but the two tables were separated by a sea of mud. We had to choose which table to visit. The student and I chose the food table! He was quite amazed to see all the hors d'oeuvres on plates where he could help himself. He wrapped some in a napkin to take home for his breakfast.

Front entrance to my townhouse

Good-bye party in my backyard

Afterwards, I asked Syntax, my regular driver and friend (on Syntax, see Chapters 3, 4 and 7), to drive the student to his aunt's place where he lived and then me back to Binnis. The aunt lived on an unpaved street, and Syntax's car was soon covered in mud. That was the only time I ever gave Syntax a tip. Later, as I got to know him, that would have been inconceivable.

Vignette: That student did his term in Maastricht and came back to Botswana to complete his BA in Political Science. After the (paid) government internship which many students do after they graduate, he applied for and was granted a full scholarship for graduate studies at the Central European University in Budapest. A fellow parishioner at the Lutheran Church in Gaborone contributed a return ticket to Budapest, since Batlang came from a modest background and could not have afforded the fare. In Hungary, Batlang fell in love with a gypsy girl. With his MA, he is now a lecturer at UB, and the gypsy girl is just a fond memory.

But back to Binnis. Besides the couple from Belfast, there was a theology professor from Ghana, Cephas, with whom I kept in touch for some time, and a law professor from Zimbabwe called Jim, who managed to stay on at UB. He is still there (2015.) He was interested in doing his PhD in international trade law, a field in which I am also interested. Since we did not have desks in our rooms, in the evening, Jim, Cephas and I would move to the dining room where each of us could occupy one large glass table and do our lecture preparation or marking or whatever it was we needed to do.

Sometimes there were other interesting guests at Binnis. Besides psychologists and nurses from Zimbabwe looking for work in Botswana — this was the time when the Zimbabwean economic crisis was at its worst — I remember a civil servant from nearby Swaziland who was working on international trade issues. She confirmed what I had suspected for some time: all the free trade areas that governments are talking about will only benefit the larger, richer countries. Countries like Swaziland do not have the expertise to calculate rules of origin or to check what comes in. It is not that this lady was ignorant, but she knew enough to know that Swaziland did not have the expertise to administer participation in a free trade area.

But all good things do come to an end. Marion and Harold were the first to leave Binnis. As a medical professor, Harold had more pull than the rest of us. No university flat being available, he was given a flat in a fancy complex of privately owned furnished flats. There Harold and Marion had everything, including a swimming pool for the complex and a television and toaster in their flat. I did phone to enquire what it would cost to live there; it cost the equivalent of about $1500 a month; that medical school did not come cheap.

Cephas managed to get a UB flat when his wife and three children came from Ghana to spend a term with him. Jim's wife wasn't sure whether she wanted to stay in Zimbabwe or move to Botswana. Eventually she and their one-year-old son did come, but she did not stay long. She left, leaving the child behind. UB assigned Jim a small townhouse not far from mine, and he coped well as a single father, taking the little boy to the daycare that the home economics students operated at UB. Eventually the wife returned; the little townhouse now is full of Jim, the wife and three children.

Finally in early December 2008 it was my turn to leave Binnis. My department chair was absolutely fantastic. He knew that one of the professors was returning to Nigeria, and somehow he managed to convince the university housing department to let me have his house, so that the house would stay in the department, so to speak, a trick I was unable to repeat when I left four years later.

Though I was glad to move to a place where I could make my own food, I did have some regrets on leaving Binnis. Unfortunately, Binnis, which was only two or three years old, did not survive for more than a year after my departure. First the management refused to take in any more bookings from the University because UB did not pay its bills on time. Then, I think it must have been in early 2010, the government shut the whole place down. The front gate was locked, the windows shuttered. There it was: a nice new bright building all closed down. I never did find out what happened. One story I heard was that the government did not want bed-and-breakfasts which did not serve evening meals, but that did not make much sense as there were other B&Bs in Botswana. Another story was that the ultimate owner was not a citizen of Botswana. The hotel and lodging sector is reserved for "citizens", a restriction which did not apply to restaurants and supermarkets and just about everything else. Even that was hard to believe because the man who said he was the owner gave me a lift to the News Café one night, and he certainly appeared to be local, though I suppose he could have been from a neighbouring country. (Fortunately, Binnis reopened in 2015.)

> *Background information: The local ownership rules were invoked from time to time in a rather arbitrary fashion. South African hotel chains are not allowed to operate in Botswana. At one time Holiday Inn managed to obtain a franchise but before the newly built hotel could open, it changed hands. A similar story is that of a walled shopping complex, called Oriental Plaza, where one could buy Chinese imports, such as luggage, household linens, shoes, and some furniture for much less than the local shops charged, even those that were Chinese-owned. During my last year in Gaborone, the government ruled that the Oriental Plaza should be limited to wholesale trade. That could not have helped the local merchants much, because Chinese-owned shops selling similar goods soon appeared on the road just outside the gate of Oriental Plaza.*

The Nigerian whose house I took over had four children, and he had hoped that his wife and children would come to join him. But his wife did not want to stay in Botswana, or perhaps she could not get a job there. The Botswana government as well as UB are very bad when it comes to giving jobs and/or visas to spouses. The Nigerian's wife was a professor of education, as was Marion, the lady from Belfast; but she could not even find anyone in the Education Faculty to talk to her and look at her résumé, let alone consider her for a job.

For whatever reason, the Nigerian professor's family went back to Nigeria. So after a couple of years in Botswana, he decided to go back too. He had furnished his townhouse with most of what a family needed, and he wanted to sell the contents of the house to me. This seemed like a good idea, except that the Nigerian wanted an impossible amount of money for his stuff. And some of the really useful things, like the pots and pans and the refrigerator, he decided to take back to Nigeria with him, though he left a little gas stove attached to a propane tank (for an inflated price, of course).

In Botswana, West Africans have a reputation for unfair dealing and greed, and Prof. O. certainly lived up that stereotype. He refused to budge on any of the prices he had set, demanding almost as much as he had paid three years earlier. I demurred, saying that I needed to wait for my husband who would be arriving from Canada in a few days. Parkash is known as a consummate bargainer, and I thought that he might be able to deal with the man. But even Parkash could make not make him budge.

I finally decided to fight back by refusing to take some of the stuff that was most outrageously overpriced. I told him to take away the dining room table and chairs because they were flimsy, like the folding tables and chairs you find in Canadian church halls. And I told him to take his television for which he wanted 1100P, even though I could buy a new Chinese-made one for 900P. I also told him to keep a ragged piece of cloth that he called a kitchen curtain, for which he wanted 200P. I had hoped that faced with the inconvenience of removing some of his stuff that he might budge on some of the rest, but he did not.

I was lucky. I found a nice pine-wood dining set for a reasonable price, and the so-called kitchen curtain, I replaced with a real, new one for 40P. We bought a 900P television from one of the local Chinese stores, and the store even replaced it when it broke down a few months later. Prof. O. had the nerve to complain to me before he left that no one would buy his television and that he was forced to donate it to his church. I would have bought it for a reasonable price. (Did I mention that Professor O. was a devout Roman Catholic who went to mass several times a week?)

The university house into which I moved was a basic townhouse, with a big backyard and a front yard where two cars could have parked except that a nice big shade tree had grown there; the roots of that tree left room for only one car. The house had been cheaply built more than twenty years ago, but it had all the basics: hot water, one and a half bathrooms and three good-size bedrooms. There was no air conditioning, but the trees in the front and the back kept the house reasonably cool (with the aid of a couple of fans) on all but the hottest days. At the front there was a metal fence and a large gate, which I had to keep locked. The gate was closed with a heavy iron chain and midsized padlock. Prof. O had seen fit to take with him not only the lock, but the chain. Did he take it to Nigeria with him? The first thing we had to do when we moved in was to get Syntax to drive us to a hardware store to buy another chain. (Parkash was visiting at that time.)

There was a second pedestrian-sized gate which separated the main front yard from a smaller yard just in front of the house where there was a laundry sink and clothes-hanging pole. (Professor O. did not take that with him!) He had also put a second lock on that small gate, but I did not fancy having to unlock two gates and the front door when I came home. So I did not bother with that second gate, and no one ever tried to break into my house from the front. Nevertheless, the University saw fit to add barbed wire to the top of both fences, which really did not make much sense because an intruder could have climbed over the gates, where there was no barbed wire...

I soon learned to keep the outside gate locked, even when I was home during the day on the weekends. If I left it open, the occasional person would wander in from the street and come to the house asking for work or money.

I became quite fond of that house; it was my connection to Botswana, my own home with my own yard.

Best of all, it was walking distance from the University. Prof. O. had pointed me in the direction of the University and the way he walked, but that was quite far. So I at first took a combi to UB. (On combis or mini-buses, see Chapter 3.) Then my friend Bayapo came by one day to see the house, and she showed me a shortcut down a back road which ran past a fancy complex of expensive-looking flats called Bokamoso (future) and then past a cemetery that had been the white people's cemetery in colonial days. It was no longer used and was surrounded by a fence without a gate, but the fence was one through which even I could climb. The city council would let the weeds around the graves grow quite high, but the respect for the dead was such that when the weeds got tall, the city finally cut them.

I visited the cemetery a couple of times. The graves included some going back to Boer War days. It was sad to see how many people had died at a young age.

The next complex, after the cemetery, was the Ministry of Transport. It was located on this out-of-the-way road so that it could be used for driving tests. After the Ministry, the road was no longer paved, making it impassable to pedestrians on rainy days. The unpaved road continued for about the length of a city block before it became a strip of grass which in turn led to a gate into the university grounds, one designed especially for construction equipment because there was plenty of building going on at UB. This gate was quite convenient for me, because it was not far from the Social Science Building where my office was.

At breakfast and again at lunchtime, enterprising locals sold cooked food to both the Ministry of Transport employees and the construction workers from cars or vans or tables that were set up along the grassy strip next to the road and outside the construction gate. I thought that I should try that food one day, but locals warned me against it. A lot of it consisted of dishes we would not normally eat, such as chicken hearts, for example.

The pedestrian gate next to the construction gate was usually open, even on the weekends, but it must have been locked some of the time, because one Monday morning when I arrived at the gate, it was locked. To the right and left of me construction workers were climbing out over the fence to get food, and students were climbing in to go to their classes. But the fence was at least five feet high, and though several students offered to help boost me over it, I declined, especially as I was wearing a skirt that day.

So I stood there like an idiot, wondering what to do next. I was too far gone to walk back to the combi stop, and the walk along the fence to the next gate was quite long, and it was getting hot. Finally I called Syntax, who, fortunately was in his office inside UB. He laughed and came to get me and drove me right to my office, saying that this one was a freebie. I did not have to put it on the monthly account.

When I arrived in my office, I phoned Security to complain about the locked gate. They told me that the man with the key had gone to his village for the weekend and had not yet come back. How Botswana!

Living in my house, I became subject to the vagaries of the University Maintenance Department.

Now people who write about living in another country almost always seem to devote pages to their encounters with the local tradesmen, be they carpenters, painters or stonemasons. It may be that middle-class people have a fascination with people who do real work, with their hands. I mean, have you ever been at a dinner party where someone asked, "How did the renovations on your house go?" and the respondent replied, "Very well, thank you. The work was done on time and according to the estimate." Now that would be the end of the conversation.

In faraway lands, contact with working people has an additional fascination. The people doing the travelling are almost invariably middle-class folks, and the working people they come in contact with are local people who do manual labour. Add in the cultural differences and the varying expectations that people in different countries have of those who belong to a different social class, and you have a mixture that can lead to some fascination and consternation.

The UB-owned houses, like rental properties anywhere, were the responsibility of the landlord. The system was supposed to work through the filtering mechanism of a Housing Manager to whom we the tenants were to bring work orders, filled out in triplicate on that nice modern carbon paper that does not have any black sheets between the pages. We were to fill out the forms and keep the pink copy and leave the white and yellow copies with the Housing Manager who was supposed to pass them on to the Maintenance Department who would then schedule the work.

It was Parkash who discovered during those first few weeks in the house that the white and yellow forms left with the Housing Manager stayed in his office. He was a busy man; he had to inspect major problems in all university properties, and he was a full-time minister in a church about thirty kilometres south of Gaborone. So Parkash developed another system which worked somewhat better. He took the work orders straight to the Maintenance Department. If he went there in the mornings, before breakfast time, that would usually bring a maintenance team to the house within a couple of hours.

I developed a routine for when there were repairs to be done. I would get Syntax to drive me to the Maintenance Department in the morning, before Botswana breakfast time. There I was greeted by the receptionist, a tall lady of traditional stature (to borrow a phrase from Alexander McCall Smith), a lady who wore a turban and a long skirt. She was always pleasant and helpful. I would fill out the work order and leave it with her, taking the precious pink copy with me. If the head of Maintenance was there, I would exchange a few words with him, an engineer who had studied in Germany and liked to practice his German. From there I could walk across the campus to my office, stopping at the better staff cafeteria for a coffee. I actually came to enjoy those morning visits.

Background fact: Alexander McCall Smith is a best-selling author, who has written a series of fifteen novels, set in Botswana. See the reading list at the end of Chapter 8.

Later that morning or the next day, two — it was always two — men would arrive to assess the situation at the house. They would promise that someone else would come to do the actual job. They might promise for that afternoon or the next morning, but it did not really matter since that second group of workers almost never arrived at the promised time. This caused me the maximum amount of inconvenience, as I either had to rush back and forth from the office on the combi or arrange for Sarah and Jason to sit in the house and wait for the workers. If I was lucky, the maid would be there, but there was only one chance in five (Monday to Friday) that that would be the case.

When the promised workmen did not arrive, I often had to make repeated calls to Maintenance and sometimes even visit there a second time before they finally came. And the work they did was substandard by anyone's standards. For example, they would paint bare surfaces without putting any primer underneath.

Two encounters with Maintenance stand out in my memory. The first was all about rats. I had only been in the house a few months when I noticed a small animal scurrying around at night time, running from upstairs down into the kitchen, looking for food. It seems that in Botswana rats live in trees, and there was a tall tree in my backyard not far from the bathroom window. A water pipe ran from the outside into the upstairs bathroom, and where the pipe penetrated the wall, there was space between the wall and the pipe, a space wide enough for a rat to squeeze through.

The short-term solution to this problem was to keep the bathroom door shut. With nothing to eat except bits of soap, the rats would not find their visits worthwhile. But this was not a long-term solution. Visitors especially might not always remember to keep the door shut.

One day I must have forgotten to close the door, because when I came home, a rat darted from the kitchen to the living room. It had been one of the nights of my evening class, so that I had come home with Syntax, not on the combi. Syntax was still outside, playing with his phone, figuring out where he was going next. I called to him to come in.

He came and with a glint in his eyes said, "I am going to kill that rat." We closed the living room door so as to imprison the rat. Next we hunted around for a killing implement, except that my house was not equipped for rat killing. Syntax rejected a cleaver and finally settled on a large wooden spoon as the best available weapon. He went into the living room, tied the bottom of the curtains into knots, so that the rat had no place to hide and then beat it to death before disposing of it outside. Good old Syntax!

Obviously I needed better rat control than a closed bathroom door. So I made a morning trek to Maintenance. Maintenance agreed that rats were a serious problem and that the best solution would be to build a wooden box around the pipes where they came in from outside, so that the rats could not get into the rest of the house. But lying on the floor to build the box was not something the Maintenance carpenters fancied doing. So they persuaded the boss that this job required hiring an outside company, who duly came and built the box and even painted it.

The day of the box building, I let the men in and went to work. When I came back at lunchtime, the gate was open, and there was a man sleeping in my front yard. He had folded his jacket and put it on the roots of the tree to make a pillow. My first fear was that this was a vagrant and that the workers had left without locking the gate. But no. He was one of the workers. The others had gone to another job and now were late in coming to pick him up.

So the box was built, and at night-time I could hear a frustrated rat or two scurrying around inside, unable to get into the rest of the house. Sometimes I would kick the box, just to let them know who was boss.

But, of course, the pipes still had to pass from the box to the toilet and the bathtub, and there was a small space between the wood and the water pipe as it left the box. One day a rat managed to squeeze through that small space, but in the process injured itself so badly that it died on the bathroom floor. That at least was my explanation for the dead rat that I found on my bathroom floor with bits of blood scattered around.

Time to contact Maintenance! As per the routine, I went in the morning and asked for a carpenter, and a couple of hours later two men showed up to assess the situation. I explained that they needed to nail a small board over the opening on top of the pipe. Well, they said it would be difficult to work on the floor underneath the sink to nail a board. Couldn't I just stuff some rags into the aperture? I asked if crumpled newspapers would do. No, they said. The rats could chew their way through newspapers, but they would not eat rags. Obviously these guys had been there before.

Now if I had wanted to stuff the aperture with rags, I would not have called for a carpenter. But who was I to judge? I did as I was told. And that was the end of rats in the house.

I had one other major encounter with Maintenance. On a Friday afternoon, when I came home around 5:00 pm, on a perfectly dry and sunny day, I found water dripping down from the frame above the entrance door. The water was accumulating on the floor and showed no signs of disappearing. So for this one and only time, I called an emergency number with which Housing had supplied me. It did not take long for three or four guys in Maintenance uniforms to show up. This was after working hours on Friday, and they would be paid overtime.

They came in and peered at the water dripping down. "Big problem! Mathatha thata!" they said. Well, yes, I knew that already. The water kept accumulating. Finally, seeing no solution coming from those guys, I phoned my husband in Canada. He said, "Did you turn off the water to the house?" Well, no, I had not thought of that, but it seemed an obvious short-term solution. I went out to the front yard and turned off the water where it came in from the city mains.

In the meanwhile, my friends from Maintenance had done some phoning of their own, and soon *the* Housing Manager himself appeared. I could see a good chance when there was one. I convinced the manager that he could not expect me to stay in a house with no water. So he authorized a hotel stay for one night. I packed up my laptop and a few essentials and called Syntax to drive me to the Planet Lodge, the hotel that the University was using since they had fallen out with Binnis. (Lodge is Botswana-speak for a small hotel or a bed-and-breakfast.)

When we arrived at the Lodge and Syntax helpfully carried my little suitcase to the front desk, the receptionist on the other side was under the impression that he had come to spend the night with me. After Syntax and I had disabused her of that notion, I settled in for the night. The lodge had stopped serving the evening meal, but they made me a grilled cheese sandwich and a nice salad and brought the food to my room, where I was also able to make a cup of tea. And the lodge had free internet. So this was a nice little break.

Before ten o'clock in the morning, the Housing Manager phoned. The water leak had been fixed temporarily, he said, and I could go back home. I don't know what produced this miracle of fast and effective work, whether it was the lure of overtime or a private company, but when I got home, someone had broken the plaster over the door, revealing two pipes connected at a right angle. It was that connection that had come loose and had been leaking. Now it had been patched together.

It took another five to six weeks of more plumbing, plastering and finally painting before the job was done to Maintenance's satisfaction, if not mine. They did not bother to paint over the plaster inside the utility closet. I complained, but to no effect. No one at Maintenance could see the point of painting where only the maid and I would see it.

Now I must, in all fairness, not paint all the workmen in Botswana with the same brush. When my television broke down, one of the drivers found me a TV repairman who was just a whiz and managed to make it work again several times, though he took quite a while to do so. When I dropped a necklace down the bathroom sink, I called a plumber who advertised in the local paper, and he found my necklace in short order. Mind you, both those guys charged lots of money, and they were immigrants from Zimbabwe.

Batswana have a passion for house building. Many of the people I knew were putting aside a part of their salary every month to build a house somewhere. My neighbours were building a fancy new house in a suburb; my colleague Dorothy and her husband were building a house in another suburb; a single young colleague was building a small house in a nearby suburb, so that he could rent it out; my friend Nobantu was building a house in a village near Gaborone, to rent out till she retired and settled there. All of these people seemed reasonably satisfied with the work that was being done, and as far as I could tell most of the workers were local. No, University Maintenance was in a class by itself. And I don't know how they got that way and what is more, how they stayed that way.

Whether you live in a house or an apartment in Botswana, you need a maid to wash your clothes (Washing machines are as yet quite rare; the only place I saw them was at an orphanage and at the university, where the students can wash their linens.) and to clean the house. Vacuum cleaners are also not common. Maids know how to clean even carpets without them, and they know how to wash silk blouses. I have saved a ton of money since I came back to Canada and started washing my silk blouses instead of taking them to a dry cleaners.

With the house, I inherited Nora, Prof. O's maid. (Nora is not her real name.) She was a whiz at cleaning. She got rid of the ants that invaded the house while we were travelling around Botswana, and she went to Zimbabwe over Christmas. She had worked at the French embassy and knew quite a bit about non-Tswana type of cooking. In Zimbabwe, she had trained as a seamstress. For a tidy sum of money, she made new curtains for the house, nice, big heavy insulating ones. They were so good that I had her make another set for our house in Canada.

I would come home and have lunch with Nora. She was also an excellent mother, who wanted her children to go to pre-school, except that it was unattainable on a maid's wages. If there was food left from her lunch, she took it home for the children. I bought them presents for Christmas in 2009. And I gave all my good shoes, for which my old feet had become too wide, to Nora's sister, who must have been the best-shod young Zimbabwean in Botswana.

It was around that time that I began to notice money missing from my wallet. At first, I thought I must have just forgotten what I had spent it on, but the problem persisted. So one day I ran a test. I came home from work and put my purse in its usual place behind the couch. Before leaving the office, I had withdrawn some money from the ATM on campus and put exactly five shiny new blue 100P bills into my wallet.

When I entered the house, I said to Nora, "It's hot. I am going upstairs to change into shorts." Then I took my time about it. After Nora was gone, I counted my money. There were just 400P.

I was absolutely devastated. All my life, the betrayal by someone I thought I could trust was what upset me the most. I am a trusting person. I like to trust others. It did not help any that Syntax would crow that I should never have trusted a Zimbabwean. I got on the phone to my friend Nobantu and dragooned her into coming to see me, so that I could cry on her shoulder, figuratively speaking. She was sympathetic, but also said that the Zimbabweans were a very acquisitive people.

The following week, I had to face Nora. I asked her to sit down in the living room with me. I told her about the missing money. I thought that if she apologized and said something like "I needed money for my brother's funeral and because my sister is a single, young mother." In that case, I would have given her another chance. She was such an excellent maid. But Nora did nothing of the kind. She denied that she had taken any money. So I had no choice but to let her go.

After that it was all downhill in the maid business. Syntax offered Sarah to clean the house. She did not want to take any money, but of course I paid her. She came with Jason, and because she and Syntax were 100% trustworthy, I did not have to come home for lunch, which was a huge convenience. I gave Sarah lunch money, so that she could buy something for s herself and Jason. Once in a while Syntax would drive me home and we would all have lunch together.

This was nice and sociable, but Sarah was not so great at cleaning the house. She liked to watch South African soap operas, and I really don't think she knew much more other than doing the dishes and the laundry, which she did very well. I let things go because I like an easy life, but when Wynie (On Wynie, see the next section on housemates.) came to live with me, she insisted that I make a list of tasks for Sarah, so that at least Sarah would know what we expected of her.

Sarah continued to clean the house for my tenant, Phoebe from Colorado, when I went to Canada during the winter of 2011. But then Sarah became pregnant and gave birth to Leticia in July that year.

When I came back in January 2012, I said to her and Syntax that it really would not be possible for her to clean the house with two small children in tow. So I was once again maidless. I managed with a bit of help from the teenager next door, until one day I came home from an official Foreign Ministry function with one of their drivers. He noticed that my front yard was not swept clean of weeds. Now I was of the opinion that sweeping the dusty front yard was not something that really needed doing — indeed I preferred the greenness of the weeds — but that was not the consensus in Botswana.

"Don't you have a maid?" the driver said. I had to admit that I did not. He immediately offered the services of his girlfriend. They had only one little girl, he said, and his partner could clean my house. She came, but aside from the fact that she was so obese that she could barely move and that like Sarah, she liked to watch soap operas, which cut into her working time, she called in sick every second week or so. So when I went to Canada for the holidays, I let her go.

One of the problems of finding a maid is that it is not considered a skilled job. It is assumed that any women can do it just because she is a woman. Women and young girls would approach me on the street and ask if I did not have "piece work" for them. But I wanted someone who knew the job and could be trusted.

After I came back in 2012, my friend Keletso said that she had a reliable maid who had one or two days a week free. Although Ole was also Zimbabwean, she did not have Nora's panache. But she was very good at the work and stayed with me until I left Botswana.

Maid stories are the currency of women's talk in Botswana, much as they must have been in Victorian England. My neighbour advised me to lock all valuables in one bedroom when the maid came, but that would mean that the bedroom would not get cleaned. Besides, I do not like these kinds of manoeuvres.

A maid story that happened to my friend Dorothy was both sad and funny. She had a full-time maid, who cooks and cleans for the family of mother, father and three teenagers living at home. One day her daughter went to the nearby mall and saw the maid wearing one of her dresses. The maid had just borrowed it, perhaps intending to put it back the following week.

If the rate of unemployment in Botswana goes down, perhaps the need for maids will decrease too and people will start buying those shiny new appliances in the electronics stores. I certainly would not want to live on the pittance a maid makes, but I must admit that having my house cleaned and my clothes ironed for me was a luxury I did not mind enjoying.

My memories of House 28 include the people who stayed there with me from time to time. The first one was Bayapo, an undergraduate student. She approached me one day when I was hobbling from Binnis to UB on my broken toe. She asked me if I needed any help carrying my books. It turned out soon enough that although she was friendly and helpful, she was also looking for free food.

Bayapo was then a third-year student, specializing in English literature and theology. She had very little money, only what her brother and father gave to her from time to time. Because her father was South African, she was not considered a citizen of Botswana and was thus not eligible for student grants. The previous year the human rights lawyer and novelist, Unity Dow, had lodged a human rights complaint against the Botswana law that said that citizenship could only be passed on through the father. Unity Dow won her case, which meant that the following year, Bayapo and many others became eligible for student grants.

But that year she was not.

When exam time rolled around in April, Bayapo's father said that he did not want to pay rent for the whole month. He wanted her to go stay with an uncle in a poor neighbourhood called Broadhurst. The uncle did not have electricity in his house, and by April the days were getting shorter, so that there would be little time to study. Bayapo asked if she could stay with me over the exam period, and I agreed. She was good company, and I helped her study Elizabethan literature (though she was pretty good at that herself), and I was quite interested in her African literature course. And cooking together was fun.

One Saturday, we walked to the mall and had a coffee and a muffin in the coffee shop there. She told me that this was the first time that she had ever been to a restaurant.

After the exams were over, Bayapo's brother came to pick her up and take her on a visit to South Africa, where her parents and some of her siblings lived. She promised to come back the next day to say good-bye, but she never came. At the beginning of the next term, she reappeared on campus. She had spent the summer (winter in Botswana) doing an unpaid internship working with underprivileged children, preparing them for the first year of school. I was amused and pleased to hear her say that those little Kalanga children spoke hardly any Setswana. She had to teach them, so that they could go to school. Bayapo's mother was a Kalanga, but Bayapo obviously identified as a Motswana. And when she returned for her fourth year, Bayapo had a student grant and was able to live in residence.

Background fact – The Kalanga, who speak a language similar to the Shona language spoken in Zimbabwe, make up about ten percent of Botswana's population. They constitute the only significant minority. About seventy-five percent of the people speak Setswana as their first language. There are a number of minority tribes, including the Basarwa (formerly called Bushmen), and the five percent who are called Whites, consisting of English and Afrikaans speakers as well as Indians, mostly from southern India, and Chinese, mostly from the Mandarin-speaking central part of that country. The Botswana government has, in my opinion wisely, refused to give any minority language official status. English and Setswana are the two official languages. South Africa has gone the other way and recognizes eleven official languages.

In her fourth year, Bayapo still occasionally came by the house or the office, looking for food. She graduated in 2010 but decided not to attend the graduation because of the cost of renting a gown. After graduation, she got a two-year paid internship working for the government, making identity cards, the *Omang* that every citizen is required to carry. In 2012, she returned to UB and was admitted to the Faculty of Education. She had always wanted to be a teacher, and she did successfully complete the course, but she could not find a job as a teacher. As far as I can tell from her Facebook page, she is now working for an NGO. She writes of going to mid-priced restaurants, such as Wimpy's and Nandos. And she has changed her names, first and last.

I invited Bayapo to my good-bye party since she was definitely part of my Botswana experience. She did not come. The next day she and her sister showed up looking for leftover food. They made a meal of the leftover barbecued sausages, then left without even much of a pretence at conversation. I was less than favourably impressed by this behaviour.

When I went to Canada in 2009, during the Canadian summer months, I arranged for Syntax, Sarah and Jason to stay in the house. After the break-in the previous January (See Chapter 6.), I was concerned about security, and they would be comfortable in my house, with its big yard. I did not charge them any rent, and they agreed to pay for the water, electricity and cooking gas they used.

The day that I came back, the television broke down. Syntax and Sarah had their own TV, which they had brought with them and installed in their bedroom together with a handful of DVDs. So they had not used my television all that much. Still they must have felt bad about it. I called the Zimbabwean who was a whiz at fixing TVs, but he took several days to do the repair.

The television was my companion. I ate my meals on a coffee table near the TV, watching France 24, a twenty-hour news channel that broadcast in English. That gave me lots of European, sometimes even Canadian, news. When I got bored with the way they repeated some of their cultural programs, like the one about truffles or the one about trends in decorating cupcakes, I even watched the Botswana channel, with its pro-government news. Occasionally I might take a peek at one of the South African channels, which broadcast in an amazing array of languages.

Without a television, I faced a silent and empty house. Sarah sensed this. So Syntax and Sarah stayed in the house with me until the Zimbabwean returned the TV. This was nice. We took turns cooking, and on Saturday morning I made pancakes. Of course, I bought all the groceries. That is the fate of a white face in Africa.

Wynie was my favourite housemate. She is an American born in Ghana, and she was in Botswana studying agricultural policies, which formed part of her PhD thesis for a university in Florida.

As a political scientist, she contacted our department as soon as she arrived. She was a great networker! She had arranged accommodation with an Environmental Studies professor from UB, who had studied in Florida. Back in Florida, it must have seemed ideal to have your own self-contained servant's quarters in the house of a professor. She moved in, and one day soon thereafter, Sarah and I, and Jason of course, drove her to the Oriental Plaza (Chinatown) to buy some basic household equipment, such as cooking pots and eating implements. This was when Syntax was trying to persuade Sarah to become a part-time driver and business partner (See Chapter 4.), and this trip was my idea of supporting Syntax in this endeavour.

We had a good shopping trip and loaded the trunk with Wynie's purchases. Of course, I bought something too, a nice porcelain serving bowl which only cost 25P or $2.10. The Chinese wholesalers have a good system whereby items that are not of top quality are sent to Africa. My bowl had a swatch of the silver paint used to decorate the edge underneath on the side, where it was not visible when the bowl was in use. I once read in the Canadian newspaper *The Globe and Mail* that there are Nigerian middlemen who live in Guangdong province near the coast of China and who buy and ship merchandise to Africa. I don't know if that system extends all the way to Botswana, but something similar must be in place.

To get back to our afternoon of shopping, Wynie's flat was not far from Chinatown, but Gaborone streets have a logic of their own. Sometimes I wondered if anyone, including the city council, had a map of the city, and although most streets had names, hardly anyone used them. Directions would run something like, "Take the road from the University to the hospital, then turn right at the Anglican cathedral". Wynie was not sure of the location of her apartment, and we made a number of wrong turns before we arrived at Wynie's place. It was just the beginning of the afternoon rush hour, and I came away with some admiration for Sarah's driving.

Wynie's flat was in a nice suburban house, but it was far from UB and the government offices, where she had to do most of her research. As you, my gentle reader, will learn in Chapter 3, public transit is all but non-existent in Gaborone, and there is none after 8:30 pm. Thus Wynie could not stay in the library late or go out in the evening without taking cabs, and that can start adding up.

One day, Wynie and her professor landlady had a big fight. With hindsight, I wonder if Wynie did not talk herself into that fight. In any case, she showed up in my office one Friday to say that she could not stay in that woman's house and that she had to move out on Sunday and could she stay with me. And would I come with her on Sunday to witness the packing up of her things, so that the landlady could not accuse her of taking what did not belong to her.

I had no problem with Wynie staying with me, but I had other plans for Sunday. And besides I was not about to get into a situation where I might have to confront a colleague. So I said, yes, you can stay with me, and this is how much it will cost and how we will share groceries and so on, but sorry, I can't come on Sunday. So Syntax missed his afternoon football and went and moved Wynie's stuff and became her witness too.

Wynie was a great housemate. We bought food when we felt like it, and sometimes cooked together, and sometimes not. And both being political scientists, we were able to discuss each other's work. And we went out to restaurants together with our laptops to catch up on our email (since my house did not have an internet connection but the restaurants did).

We had fun. We walked over to the old white folks' cemetery which I had not yet visited and Wynie posed sitting on top of tombstones. She and my colleague Dorothy and I went out to fancy overpriced coffee shops, since Dorothy had a car to take us to those places. It is one thing to pay 20P ($2.80) for a latte; another to pay 60P for cab to take you to and from that coffee shop. On Wynie's fortieth birthday we went to one such coffee shop for cake and coffee and took pictures of ourselves.

After Parkash came from Canada for a visit, Wynie said she needed Christmas presents for the family reunion her husband had planned for Sweden that Christmas of 2010. I knew a graduate student who wanted to make a bit of extra money by taking us to the countryside to visit some potteries. December is mid-summer, and it was a hot, sunny but enjoyable day. The first pottery was in a kind of artists' commune with a fence surrounding it. It included a workplace for metal-working and a kennel where people could leave their cats. (Very few people in Botswana have pet cats. Dogs are common though.) I do not remember what there was in the other buildings. Some of them were closed and appeared to be unoccupied. The pottery though was open. We had phoned ahead to make sure that there would be someone there. The shop and the pottery were run by a single mother from Zimbabwe and her three teenage daughters. The oldest was going to university, and the shop helped to pay for that. We bought a few things and drove on to the next pottery, which was started by the Roman Catholic Church as a local make-work project. Here there was much larger selection of things, all decorated in a distinctive pattern of white triangles on a deep brown background. I still have a sugar bowl I bought there. I did not want to buy anything that would be too big to carry to Canada, but that did not seem to bother Wynie, who bought some bowls to take to Sweden.

In spite of the heat, it was a pleasant afternoon.

Wynie had her quirks. She seemed to be a preferred target for thieves, and she also lost many of her possessions. When she first came to Botswana, she had almost no clothes because her two suitcases had been stolen when she changed planes in Kenya. Someone managed to deprive Wynie of the charger for her Apple computer while she was working in the UB library, and that turned out to be a big problem because at that time Botswana did not have an Apple store. (It does now.) She lost her jacket and running shoes, and accused the girl next door of taking them. Now that girl did turn out to be a thief, but even when I caught her stealing from me, she insisted that she had not taken Wynie's stuff. I believed her because she was mainly after money and alcohol, not clothing.

When Wynie returned to Botswana in 2011, while I was in Canada looking after some medical issues of my own, she had once again to travel to Kenya, and there someone stole her laptop while she fell asleep on a bus. Wynie complained to the bus driver who told her that she should not have been sleeping. I thought: why didn't she put the laptop under her feet.

Perhaps Wynie should have stayed away from Kenya. After she arrived, she duly applied to study agricultural policy. The authorities not only refused her that permission; after the government received her request, someone from the president's office sent security personnel to her lodging to escort her to the airport and thus out of the country.

When I cleared out my house in December 2012, I found a box at the very back of the storage room underneath the stairs. It was full of Wynie's possessions. There were some cosmetics, a couple of dresses and books and some sewing supplies, her camera, which she thought she had lost in northern Botswana, a fancy silk camping sheet which had been a present from her in-laws, plastic braces for her teeth that she was supposed to wear at night, and a white silk-bound family Bible with a gilded edge.

I consulted Wynie as to what to do with all that stuff. I was able to send a few of the small, light and valuable things to Florida with a Botswana student who was travelling there. The rest I gave away, except for the camera which is now in our house in Toronto. Parkash got it working with a charger he bought from Kodak. I don't want to mail it across the border; I will send it to Wynie when next one of us travels to the US.

Wynie had one other characteristic that in the minds of those of us who sometimes like to stereotype others marked her as a West African. She was an inveterate bargainer. When we went to the health food store in Riverwalk, she picked out what she wanted, then started asking for discounts, always beginning her sentence with "I am a student." She did the same at the potteries, and it actually worked! Luckily she did not try to bargain with me about the rent.

Wynie and I had planned to leave for Johannesburg together and have Syntax drive us to Johannesburg, but her husband managed to find some deep discount flight to Sweden which left a week earlier. So Wynie had to fly on her own, as did I. I have not seen Wynie again, though we are still in occasional email contact. And I do have her camera.

My last housemates were two ladies from China, a professor of education and her research assistant. Because there is a shortage of accommodation in Gaborone, when the two ladies came and I was in Canada due to a medical problem, the man who ran the international office asked whether he could put them into my house. They were still there when I returned in January 2012.

At first I did not feel very comfortable with them. They kept their food strictly separate from mine, cooking voluminous stir-frys in my largest frying pan, and the professor particularly was dour and unpleasant. She pretended that she hardly understood any English, which was not true. She was also quite mean and bossy toward the research assistant. I imagined her to be some kind of Communist party apparatchik.

The Chinese professor was very careful with money. She insisted that the two of them must always walk to the University and not take the combi, even when it was boiling hot outside, or even worse when it was raining. On a rainy day the two of them would come back with muddy shoes that they would have to wash. I did not walk when it rained because part of the road was not paved, and I would not walk during the hottest part of the day.

I solved the food problem by making some Chinese food for myself one day. The ladies looked at my little stir-fry and said, "Look, she knows how to make that kind of food too." After that, we did sometimes share our food. But when they left, they packed up all of their groceries and gave them to some Chinese people in another UB house nearby. I was left with a half bottle of soy sauce that they probably forgot about.

The young research assistant was a pleasant person, and as the time for the ladies' departure came near, she showed some independence from her boss. Two weeks before they left, Botswana went into a football (soccer) paroxysm during the finals of the Africa Cup. By a miracle, Botswana had qualified to place in the finals. When the national team played its first game, the whole country stopped whatever it was doing, and everyone found him- or herself a television to watch. I went to a local pub. The Chinese ladies stayed home. But when it was time for the second game, the research assistant, said she wanted to see the game and the local people's reaction to it. So we walked to a pub in the mall, it still being daylight, and came back with Syntax, who was watching the game at the same pub. It was obvious that Madame Professor disapproved of this going off to a pub, but Wei did not let that bother her. (Botswana lost all three games and was eliminated from the finals.)

Wei must be from a wealthy family. She travelled with her laptop, but told me that she also had an iPad at home and that she did not want to bring both with her. She also had a younger brother, another sign of wealth because in the cities in China an urban family has to pay a stiff fine to have a second child. One Sunday, my friend Dorothy took me to mass at the Roman Catholic cathedral downtown because I wanted to see the bilingual service. The next Sunday, Wei told me that she had never seen the inside of a church, much less a church service, and would I take her? Since Dorothy was not available, we set off just the two of us, once again under the disapproving eyes of Madame. A mass is a mass, wherever you are, and I had picked up some religious vocabulary by then. The two of us managed to get through the mass without becoming too much of an embarrassment, and the locals, who must have found us a strange addition to their congregation, did not stare at us too much.

Wei and her boss had a small camera for taking pictures of documents. They were studying post-secondary education in Botswana, and they accumulated a pile of calendars, course catalogues and publicity pamphlets from the institutions they visited. A couple of days before they left, Wei photographed every page of the material they had collected, leaving me with a pile of useless paper. (Gaborone does not as yet recycle paper.)

> *Factual aside: Gaborone is supposed to provide weekly garbage pickup, and most of the time that works just fine. But some Tuesdays, the garbage truck did not show up, and sometimes it did not come two Tuesdays in a row. This resulted in overflowing garbage cans — each household was allowed just one — and garbage blowing all over the street, which brought more than the usual number of little gray monkey scavengers.*

Wei and I are still Facebook friends. After she returned to China, she spent a term at a Danish university, and from there she went to the OECD in Paris for two months. She did not update her Facebook page for more than a year after she left the OECD. Early in 2015, she reappeared on Facebook. She is now a government official in Beijing, which apparently allows her to access Facebook.

When the time for my return to Canada approached, I knew that I would have to throw some kind of a good-bye party for my Batswana friends. There would be at least forty to fifty people to invite, and the thought of doing something at the house was quite intimidating. I started checking out local restaurants, but the ones that were good were terribly expensive, and the others all had problems: they were either far from anywhere or in an unsafe neighbourhood.

Along came Tebogo, a former graduate student of mine. We had made an occasional meal together or gone to a movie, but I had been paying for everything — African style. I had seen her less often since she got married in 2011. (I was unable to attend the wedding because I was in Canada all of that year,) When I came back I invited her and her new husband out to a dinner at a restaurant of their choice. Tebogo was modern enough to appreciate such a post-materialist wedding present. Herbert is a police detective who specializes in fingerprints. He is also taking business courses because they are hoping to start a business of their own.

Anyway, I bumped into Tebogo while I was agonizing about the location of the party. She was a court clerk at the Magistrate's Court near my house. She immediately took charge of the dossier. She said that she had planned many events for her church, that she knew where to order good finger food and where to rent tables and chairs and how to find a DJ and that I should hold the party in my own backyard, which would be a lot cheaper and probably more fun too than sitting in a restaurant.

I found the idea of a party in the backyard most appealing, not only because it would save money. The yard is, after all, the centre of family life in Botswana. Weddings and funerals and other family celebrations are held there. One of the weddings we attended took place in a rented hall, though the family had a perfectly good yard where I had attended a tombstone unveiling celebration the year before. People's attitudes were that the newlyweds were showing off; weddings are held in the *yard*, with awnings above in case it rained. There is a good Setswana word for house, *ntlo*, but it only refers to the physical building. There is another word, *lolwapa*, which means family or home or yard, depending on the context. So I was most anxious to have my party in the yard, like a true Motswana.

With Tebogo's help it was all arranged. Of course, she and I had lots of help. I panicked when I realized that on the date I had chosen for the party, December 7, Syntax would be in Pretoria playing soccer, but I recovered from the panic and drew on all the resources I could muster.

Tebogo looked after the food, except what people brought themselves. She did everything she had promised to do and stayed to help the whole evening. I had some concerns about her because the week before she had told me that she was pregnant and suffering from morning sickness. I talked my friend Tom from Serowe into coming down for the weekend and staying at the house and helping out, which he did in spades. My backup driver, Robert, agreed to pick up the food and do any other necessary driving, which included picking up Sarah and the children; (All three of them were with her that week.) and bringing them over to the party. I did want them to be there, as they had been such an important part of my Botswana experience. Sarah had the car, but understandably she did not want to drive in the dark with three children.

Maybe it was just as well that Robert instead of Syntax was doing the driving. Syntax would have had his own ideas on how to run the party. Robert did what I asked.

Finally the time for the party rolled around. It was 7:00 pm on December 7. Everyone had been so helpful. A colleague, Gladys, drove me to a factory run by some people from India that made plastic dishes and glasses. So I was able to buy everything wholesale. The neighbours lent me plastic tubs to hold the ice on which to cool the beer. The neighbours' daughter brought one of her school friends, and they helped serve the food. (One fringe benefit for them was that they were able to partake of the wine and beer, which they were not allowed to have at home.) And Boniface, one of my officer students from the BDF, brought 4 kg of boerwors, the mildly spiced South African-style sausage that is made especially for barbecuing.

There were a few hitches, of course. The political science secretary insisted on making papa (cornmeal porridge). She brought a huge cauldron and cooked it on my stove, but hardly anyone ate it, and the next day we had to feed it to the neighbours' dogs. She also used up all my remaining cooking gas. The neighbours' daughter had said that she could borrow a barbecue and I had bought charcoal, but when Boniface arrived with the boerwors, there was no barbecue, and dear Gladys drove across town to borrow her sister's. When Gladys got back, another colleague, Keb, and Tom and Boniface gathered around the barbecue and cooked the sausages. I loved the red glow of the charcoal in the dark backyard. The sausages were delicious when they were cooked, but by that time people had eaten most of the rest of the food. When one graduate student, a Rastafarian and thus a vegetarian, arrived late, there were only sausages and papa left to eat.

I had wanted there to be a short program, where people — and I — could speak. I asked Beth, another former graduate student, to be the MC. She is a really nice person, a rather big girl both ways, and she has a deep booming voice. She arrived at the party accompanied by another woman. Good for her, I thought, but then she introduced the other woman as her boyfriend's mother! I did not believe a word of it, of course.

Beth was a great MC, and since I don't like listening to speeches, I kept the list short and gave everyone a maximum of ten minutes, but hardly anyone used that much. I chose Nobantu as a former graduate student and good friend, a former undergraduate student, who spoke for only about a minute, David, the department chair, because I think that he expected to be asked. Then I spoke briefly to tell everyone how wonderful they had been to me. Beth asked if anyone else wanted to speak. Only a couple of people got up: my neighbour, the father of the girl Mpho who had given me so much trouble (see the chapter on crime) and Dr. Maipose, who had been department head when I was hired. He made the best comment of all. He said that after he came to the airport to meet me when I first arrived, he thought, "She won't last two months." And yet I stayed for more than three years.

I have one regret. I had asked Nobantu to write me a couple of sentences in Setswana, so that I could say a few words in that beautiful and descriptive language, but that afternoon I was busy with all kinds of arrangements for the party and did not manage to learn that part of my speech. That was one of those missed opportunities that cannot be made up, like the fathers' day at the prenatal classes that I missed because I had a research commitment that day. That was in 1970. Obviously, I do not have many great regrets.

After the speeches and the food, the DJ and his helper set up shop and people started to dance. I have a wonderful picture of my friends and colleagues dancing in a circle, African style, while the barbecue glowed in the background.

I had bought lots of beer and wine and soft drinks for the party, and in the process I learned that wine is cheap and beer is expensive in Botswana. I did not buy anything stronger, partly because of the cost and the hassle of mixing drinks but mostly because I did not want trouble with guests who had imbibed too much. Tom told me after the party that some of the guests, especially the military officers, brought their own drinks and went out to their cars to drink. Fortunately I did not notice that at the time.

Background fact: Wine and sometimes beer are sold in the better supermarkets. Beer is also available from so-called bottle stores; these are seedy places that I would not enter. All kinds of alcohol are sold in special privately owned liquor stores that are scattered around the city. Traditional and homemade beer is also sold in illegal pubs called shebeens, which are tolerated by the police.

The officers in the two classes I had taught became an issue. I had invited all eight of the graduate students, but from the larger undergraduate class — there were 28 of them — I had invited only the class president, who was the person with whom I was supposed to communicate for the whole class, and one officer, Boniface, whom the BDF had sent to Canada to learn French and who liked to practise what was left of his French by speaking to me. (Boniface was his real name, not a French-Canadian name he had adopted at the Collège militaire royal de Saint-Jean.) But word got around, and before long I learned that all of my BDF students were planning to attend. I panicked, especially after I ran into Elijah, one of the officers from the undergraduate class in the local supermarket, and he gave me a big grin with his large teeth, one of which was missing: "I hope you have bought lots of beer."

> *Vignette — for the duration of the term, the officers taking the undergraduate course were housed in the civil service college, which happened to be within walking distance from my house. The classes were held there too, which was certainly more convenient than being driven out to the BDF College on the northwest outskirts of the city. Sometimes I would run into some of the officers at the local supermarket, where they came to buy food to supplement their rations or stationery and toiletries. I saw Elijah there frequently, to the point where once I mentioned that maybe he should spend some time studying. But I guess Elijah knew what he was doing. He did quite well in the course.*

> *Fact — At independence, there were no dentists in Botswana. There are some now — there is even an orthodontist in Riverwalk — but people do not have the habit of going to them. Many people have teeth missing, especially the men. I don't know if this is because they fear dentists or because of the cost of dental work, which is not covered by government health insurance.*

Back to the party! Only a dozen or so officers showed up; most of them spent that weekend with their families in various parts of the country. So my worries about dozens of officers drinking beer proved unfounded.

The music played on, and I had to pose for individual pictures with several of the guests. I had experienced this before. People did not just want pictures; they wanted individual pictures of themselves with the person being honoured. At the end of the graduate course at the BDF College, someone produced a BDF photographer who took a class photo; then I had to pose with each one of the eight officers.

At midnight, the music stopped. Exasperated dancers converged on the DJ. He explained that Tebogo had only booked and paid him for four hours. Finally he agreed to play for one more hour. But then some of the would-be dancers started complaining about the music. Now it was the DJ's turn to be exasperated. He packed up and left, and soon the guests began to leave too. I must admit that I was relieved. There is a certain macho quality to partying in Botswana. Invitations usually give a starting time, say eight o'clock, followed by the ominous words "till late", meaning until the last guest drops from exhaustion, which could be at three or four in the morning.

My party was truly over by one a.m.

Tom and I locked the gate and sat down and chatted for a while over a well-deserved cup of tea. I did a quick count from memory; there had been about 72 people at the party, and, as one of the speakers pointed out, most of them were local people, Batswana from various parts of the country. The only exceptions were a few colleagues from neighbouring countries and three whites — Tom, Tresa (a sociology professor from Zimbabwe but of Irish origin), and me. Almost all of my colleagues from the Department of Political and Administrative Studies were there, including those who usually avoided departmental social functions.

> *Reality check: a note about racial terminology in Botswana: Sad to say, Batswana are extremely race conscious. It is not that they discriminate against whites or people from minority tribes (except for Basarwa — formerly known as Bushmen, the indigenous people of Botswana — and Zimbabwean immigrants. Discrimination against these two groups is rampant.) White persons are treated with deference but also a kind of fascination. They are routinely referred to as* makgoa *(singular* lekgoa*). On one occasion a blond Canadian, briefly a tenant at my house, took my internet modem to the cell phone company and had it transferred to her cell number, without any authorization from me. I sold the same modem to a colleague when I left Botswana, and she had difficulty getting it transferred to her cell phone number, even though I had given her a signed letter to say that the modem now belonged to her. She had to email me in Canada for me to give her the passwords before the cell phone company would transfer the modem to her phone number. The most likely*

explanation for this anomaly is that the staff at the cell phone office assumed that the white Canadian student had come by the modem honestly (not true) whereas the local professor was not given the same degree of trust.

It had been an eventful, a wonderful day. The next morning, I slept in a bit later than usual and took a long shower. By the time I came downstairs, Tom had stacked most of the rented chairs in the front yard and had cleaned the backyard and living room. I offered to make him a pancake breakfast, Canadian style, but he announced that he was hung over and was going back to bed. I felt so guilty about his having done all that work; as for me, I had not taken a single drink all evening. I wanted to enjoy the evening fully, experience it as it was.

I could not have done the party without Tom and Tebogo and many others. The money I had spent on Tebogo had been repaid many times over. That is how it is in life: we give and we receive. My life in Botswana had been a little bit like that of Dr. Zhivago, except that it was much more pleasant: it would not have been possible without the help of brothers and sisters such as Tom and Tebogo, who always appeared at just the right time.

And that is how I had a real Botswana party in my *yard*.

My time in Botswana was drawing to a close. I had sold all of the furniture and curtains in the house before the party. Ole (the maid) and I covered the couches and the easy chairs and the dining room table with sheets, lest they suffer damage during the party.

As a member of the Alliance française, I had sometimes received emails from expatriates who were returning home and wanted to sell the contents of their house. I needed no such emails. Everything in the house sold itself. Friends came and asked me if they could buy the microwave or the fridge or the dining room table. I didn't sweat the small stuff. I gave to Dorothy some leftover ground coffee that a BDF officer had brought me from Rwanda, and the baking dishes went to the political science secretary who from time to time baked cakes or squares to sell. All the remaining groceries and pots and pans and dishes

I left to Ole and Sarah. In return for taking it all away and cleaning the cupboards, they could share what there was. Syntax expressed some concern that Sarah would not take her share, but when I saw them loading up the stuff, I think that Sarah had done quite well. In any case, there seem to have been no disputes.

Several people, including Tom and an American girl who had worked in Botswana for a couple of years, warned me that, knowing that I had to leave by December 19, people would not pay me for the things they had agreed to buy, but this did not happen. Everyone paid for everything exactly the amount they had promised. I was not owed a single thebe. My friends are the best friends, in Africa and in Canada.

CHAPTER 2   FOOD AND DRINK

During my first three months in Botswana, I lived in a bed-and-breakfast which did not serve any other meals. So my introduction to Botswana food consisted of a mixture of the Western and the African, well, the almost African.

On the campus of the University, there were two staff cafeterias and two huge, cavernous student cafeterias, known by the quaint British name refectories. Although it was possible for the staff to buy food from the refectories, this was almost unheard of. I popped into one occasionally to buy an ice cream or another snack in the evening, when the staff cafeterias were closed. (We were expected to teach in the evening, part-time graduate courses for people who worked during the day, but we were not expected to eat in the evening.) My sorties into the refectory inevitably attracted stares from anyone around.

On my first full day on campus, my department chair proudly took me to the nearer of the two staff cafeterias where for less than $4.00 we could buy a meal of meat, a starch, two servings of salad or vegetables, and a glass of a drink which resembled Kool-Aid. The price went up to about $4.50 over my four years in Botswana, but the food stayed pretty much the same.

Lunch was served from twelve noon to 2:00 pm, and by 1:30 the choice of foods had decreased. If you arrived between 12:55 and 1:15, there would be a long line-up. So there really was only one optimum lunchtime, 12:45. Before that, the cafeteria would be all but empty, and there would be no chance to socialize, and what good is lunch at work if you cannot socialize and gossip?

As is the case elsewhere, nearly everyone complained about the food in the cafeterias, but I do think that at UB they had good reason to do so. The main feature of lunch was the starch, which consisted of a choice of one of two or three of the following: sorghum porridge, corn porridge, rice, spaghetti and less frequently, a large yeast dumpling called *ledombi*, a different kind of corn porridge called *samp*, French fries, or steamed potatoes.

Sorghum porridge is a natural grain that might be good for us, but the taste of the porridge was what I imagined ground cardboard might taste like. Friends told me that it was better when mixed with mashed pumpkin or when fermented. Perhaps. One friend asked her maid to prepare sorghum porridge with pumpkin for me, and it had a better texture than the cafeteria version, but still was not something I would choose to eat.

Sorghum, which grows well in the harsh climatic conditions of Botswana, is the traditional staple food, but in contemporary Botswana, it has been largely replaced by a thick cornmeal porridge known as *papa*. When Syntax's partner Sarah prepared papa at my house, she stirred it many times with a kind of shortened whisk attached to a stick. Thus aerated, the papa became quite tasty and went well with a dish of chilli. The stuff served in the cafeteria was thick, like a drier version of mashed potatoes.

While I preferred papa to sorghum, I soon limited my intake of it because it packed on the pounds. It has probably also contributed to the alarmingly high incidence of diabetes in the country. I watched in amazement as colleagues piled their plates high with papa or sorghum porridge. Ditto for the rice, which many in the cafeteria preferred to the traditional starches, but which if my medical knowledge does not fail me, may also contribute to the incidence of diabetes.

In a novel set in Botswana — which is appropriately called *Mating* but which is not really about Botswana, but rather about a foreign woman who sleeps with various non-Batswana men — author Norman Rush makes a snide comment to the effect that Batswana do not feel really full unless they have eaten porridge. It is true that porridge is a traditional staple food and that in the Lord's Prayer, the word for bread is *bogobe*, meaning porridge. But the Lord's Prayer was translated a long time ago, and now people who do not have access to a cafeteria are just as likely to eat bread as a staple food. At the local supermarket I often saw construction workers coming in to buy a loaf of sliced bread and perhaps a small roll of a particularly vile-tasting cold meat called polony, and that would be breakfast for two people.

In the cafeterias, potatoes were popular and usually disappeared by 1:15 pm. Spaghetti less so, perhaps because it was served without any sauce, but since it was cheap and convenient to prepare, it was becoming a more frequent menu item.

The starches, other than potatoes, which I preferred were *samp* and *ledombi*. Samp is yet another kind of porridge, one that is prepared from the cracked grains of white corn that are cooked until they are soft and mushy and to which cooked black beans may be added. It certainly is no less fattening then papa or sorghum, but it does taste a whole lot better. Though it made an infrequent appearance at the UB cafeteria, samp remains a staple at wedding and funeral banquets.

My favourite starch was *ledombi*, a large dumpling made of white flour, yeast and water and cooked in water. The cafeteria next to the administration block, where the bigwigs ate, had slightly better food than the one near my office, and since it was only a five-minute walk from my office, that is where I would usually take my lunch. Except in the very hottest weather, I would shun the somewhat longer shady route favoured by my colleagues and cut diagonally through a parking lot, the heat burning my head. All of this to get to the weekly Monday treat of ledombi — and not incidentally to show that I could take the heat — literally.

A ledombi is supposed to be eaten with beef stew with lots of gravy to cover the dumpling. Though the cafeteria did serve the dumpling with beef stew, there never seemed to be enough gravy to go around. This is mystifying because you would think that it would be cheaper to make more gravy and less meat. And although beef, being one of the country's principal agricultural products and exports, is relatively inexpensive in Botswana, the cafeteria always ran out of stew. One day the server suggested that I eat my ledombi with chicken. Now the cafeteria chicken was a weird kind of thing, a chicken cut into small unrecognizable pieces, of which we were allotted two each. I don't know how they cooked the chicken, but it was always covered in some kind of goo which may have been intended to be a glaze, and it was bone-dry on the inside. I used to say that they must have put the chicken in a special dryer to make the inside so dry.

Traditional cooking pots

A true ledombi is huge, and I could not eat a whole one in one meal. Yet I saw some men ordering two of them at a time! I solved the problem of the large ledombi by cutting mine in half and stuffing the uneaten half into a styrofoam cup which the coffee bar staff kindly gave to me. If they were being especially nice, they even gave me a small piece of foil paper to cover the cup. If I did not forget it in the office, I took my half ledombi home and prepared some beef liver with onions, mushrooms and beef stock the next evening. Delicious.

The other kind of proteins the cafeteria served were liver, a kind of breaded fish, probably once frozen, and something thin, dry and tough they called steak. Since Botswana is far from any ocean, I stayed away from the fish, and I soon learned to avoid the steak. Once in a while, there was goat stew, and on most Fridays the more upscale of the two cafeterias served a river fish called bream. Each bream was exactly of the same size and appearance, and each was served complete with head, eyes, scales and tail; the bream came from a fish farm in the northern part of the country where there was enough water to fill a couple of rivers and presumably also supply a fish farm or two. The appearance of the bream put me off; I never did order one, though one day a friend persuaded me to try it from her plate, and it tasted pretty much like a Canadian freshwater fish, such as a whitefish.

Vegetables were the low point of cafeteria cuisine. Sometimes all we got was frozen mixed vegetables, steamed. There might also be tasteless sautéed cabbage or spinach which almost always included some sand, mashed pumpkin, a favourite with the locals, or steamed carrots. And there always was salad. Cut-up lettuce to which a few slivers of green or red pepper might have been added was there every day. Additional salads might include a red beet salad or coleslaw. Since my heritage includes pickled red beets, I tried eating them, but they inevitably gave me an upset stomach.

The green "salad" was served dry without any dressing, though toward the end of my stay, the lesser of the two cafeterias started putting out some oil and vinegar that we could sprinkle around if we wanted to. And by the way, every vegetable was known as salad, regardless of its actual state of cooking. Similarly, all cooking liquids, including gravy, were called soup, even though I never knew the cafeteria to serve soup.

Vegetarians had a tough time with the cafeteria offerings. The lesser cafeteria served vegetarian patties that could be eaten with whatever else might be available that day. Vegetarian friends assured me that the patties were totally devoid of taste. Such friends also told me that the cafeteria staff were none too helpful when it came to providing vegetarian food. On one occasion, a server at the cafeteria tried to tell my vegetarian friend Gladys that chicken was not really meat and that she should eat it.

Batswana are traditionally a beef-eating people, fond of their cattle and its meat, but there are a good number of vegetarians around. There are professors and business people from India. And there are local

Rastafarians as well as others who became vegetarian out of conviction or for health reasons. Gaborone has a good vegetarian supermarket called Mr. Veg, but none of this seems to have come to the attention of the cafeteria managers who, strange to say, are originally from India; their firm is called *Moghul*.

Though most Batswana are fond of sweets, dessert after a meal is not a local tradition. However, to cater to us foreigners and the many members of the university staff who had studied abroad, the better cafeteria included a dessert and coffee bar. There were always two desserts, a huge bowl of a trifle consisting of canned fruit salad mixed with jelly, topped by a custard, and another huge bowl of canned fruit salad with some fresh fruit mixed in. A serving filled a medium-sized soup bowl, topped by an optional covering of heavy table cream. Sometimes there was also a layer cake cut into large slices. I avoided that, but I often enjoyed the trifle, which was quite tasty though fattening. It had the good effect of covering up the taste of the main course.

Tea was just a tea bag floating in a mug, and there was choice of regular or rooibos, the "bush tea", favoured by Alexander McCall Smith's fictional heroine Mma Ramotswe. Coffee could be instant or filter. I tried the filter coffee one day and got a bitter cup of a dark liquid that must have been sitting on the heat for several hours. No Tim Horton's twenty-minute rule there. I stuck to instant coffee after that.

One peculiarity of the cafeterias was that if you departed from the standard items, say you wanted just a salad, or meat and salad and no starch, there was no way of determining what the price would be. The price fluctuated widely from day to day, One day I would pay 8P for just salad, another 12P, and there was no arguing with the person at the cash.

There were a couple of alternatives to the cafeteria. One was meat pies. At the centre of the campus, in front of the library, there stood a kiosk which sold meat pies, soft drinks and small bags of potato chips and candy bars. The meat pies were delicious and consequently usually ran out by one o'clock or so. Pie City, the country's major producer of the delicacy, made wonderful meat pies with a flaky crust and a savoury interior. Chicken and mushroom and steak and kidney were especially good. I could buy a meat pie and take it to the cafeteria and eat it with their salad. So why did I not do this every day? The meat pies were so good and so reasonably priced — 9P or about $1.30 — that there was always a long line of students waiting to be served. Botswana tradition would have allowed me as a "lecturer" to jump the queue, but I would never have done that. So it was either the line-up or the cafeteria. Besides, there was a certain camaraderie in sharing the bad cafeteria food with my colleagues.

The other alternative to the cafeteria were various food purveyors who set up shop on the streets around the campus. By the pedestrian gate, there were ladies selling long fat wieners, called russians in Botswana, together with greasy French fries. At the north gate, there were tables selling beef or chicken stew and cooked vegetables and rice and even salad, though I would never have eaten salad that was stored on a hot street. I tried the beef stew once; it was quite tasty and a little less expensive than the cafeteria's, but buying that food meant walking all the way to the gate and then back to the cafeteria with my styrofoam box. That was a fairly long trek. A student told me that there were also food dealers by the south gate and that there was, he said with astonishment, a "white guy" selling really good food, but since that was some distance from my office, I never did get to sample the white guy's food.

There was a gate for construction equipment at the eastern end of the campus, where I walked to UB in the mornings. A few ladies sold cheaper food there for the construction workers, food such as tripe or beef hearts. I always thought I should try that food one day, but I never did. My colleagues warned me against it. The cafeterias, whatever might be wrong with them, maintained high sanitary standards. All the staff wore hair nets and plastic gloves if they needed to touch any food.

During my last year at UB, a couple of takeout places opened in the new student services building, but the food there was of variable quality and tended to run out, not to mention that there were often long line-ups. In that building there was also a store selling groceries, ice cream, newspapers, and toiletries. None of these places stayed open in the evenings.

That nothing was open in the evening was a real problem for those of us who taught graduate students, who came in after a day at work. Only the kiosk was open until eight, and by that time it had run out of much of its offerings, and it was a fair distance from some of the classroom buildings. Gradually a tradition developed whereby I brought cookies to class to eat during the no-coffee coffee break. I bought several small packages of the cheapest cookies from the local supermarket and distributed them at break time. The students loved it, and it probably helped to keep them awake for what remained of the class. Once I thought I would buy a treat and brought a large bag of grapes instead of cookies. The students were disappointed, and a Rastafarian complained that he did not eat grapes.

Batswana just love cookies. Whenever I put out a plate of cookies at home to serve with tea or coffee, they all disappeared in no time. One of my friends was a retired diplomat, and I thought that she might show some restraint when it came to the consumption of cookies, but this was not the case.

In fact, Batswana are *inordinately* fond of cookies. Once I was standing in a long, slow-moving line at the government clinic near my house. I asked the man behind me if he would keep my spot if I went home to mark some papers. He was Zimbabwean. When I went back, I took a package of cookies from my cupboard to give to him. He did not want them, but the local lady in front of him gladly took them. I used to joke that if Botswana ever had a currency crisis, the money would consist of cookies for the smaller denominations and T-shirts for the larger ones.

Back to the cafeterias. The university cafeteria served breakfast as well as lunch. Breakfast in Botswana is usually eaten at 10:00 am or so. As is the case in most tropical countries, Batswana rise early and eat just a small snack or nothing first thing in the morning. The UB workday begins at 8:00 or 8:30 am, and at 9:30 or 10:00, people go to the cafeterias for a big fattening breakfast: bread, pancakes, eggs, bacon, sausages, muffins and *phapatha* washed down with tea or instant coffee. Of course, not everyone would eat all of that on any one morning; that was the range of stuff available. (A phapatha is a large baking powder biscuit, delicious when it is fresh and flaky. The ones made by the cafeteria were larger and tastier than those in the supermarkets.)

I preferred to eat breakfast at home, before I went to work, which made me late by Botswana standards, but that does not matter too much with professors when they don't have a class. I then skipped the cafeteria breakfast, though occasionally I would go with a colleague, just for the company, to enjoy a phapatha with margarine and jam (butter being a rare luxury in Botswana. The local supermarket did not even carry it.)

Once, when Syntax and Sarah were staying with me in August 2009, Syntax came home for his breakfast break, while Sarah and Jason were still having their bath. I thought he would be annoyed and say something like, "Woman, where is my breakfast?" But no. He saw that I had bought some groceries. He helped himself to a couple of eggs, scrambled them, and ate them with several slices of bread. Then he put the dishes in the sink and went back to work.

Before I leave the subject of the local food, one more story and one more observation. Nearly everyone drinks tea or coffee regularly, except for a few religious fanatics who eschew caffeine. People usually take their coffee or tea with milk — cream is all but unheard of — and sugar, lots of sugar. Most of my acquaintances added four or five teaspoons of sugar to a mug. They must have been drinking syrup, not coffee or tea.

And now the story. One Sunday morning a colleague called me and asked me to come to his place for a typical Botswana lunch. Within an hour he was there to pick me up. He showed off his beautiful suburban house with garage and rose garden. Then, as we sat on the couch, his wife knelt on the floor and offered us a bowl of warm water in which to wash our hands. We then sat at the table the colleague, his wife, two children (one a teenager, one six years old) and the maid who had prepared the meal. The maid sat at the table but did not participate in the conversation. The meal consisted of a stew of goat tripe and a stiff version of papa, so stiff that my hosts used it to pick up their meat, though I was supplied with a fork and knife. For dessert there was a watermelon with a thick skin. To drink, there was water.

I do believe that this traditional meal was a bit of a show. For one thing, the colleague's wife was a mechanical engineer who worked for the national electricity company. He was proud of her, and often boasted about his wife the engineer who was working on her MBA part-time. I doubt she usually knelt with a water bowl in her hand when the house had more than one bathroom. And I think the menu was also chosen to test me. I ate the goat tripe like a trooper; it did not taste too bad, except that it seemed to have some sandy bits in it.

Non-traditional Food

Obviously, I could not rely on the University for sustenance. Fortunately, I lived within walking distance of three and a half supermarkets, a discount supermarket that was just three minutes' walk from my house and two and half others in a nearby mall. The discount store is called Choppies and is one of a chain of stores founded by a business-man of Indian origin, who still owns a majority of the shares. Another major shareholder is Festus Mogae, a former president of Botswana. The remaining shares are listed on the miniscule Botswana stock exchange. The chain is very successful. By the time I left, they had opened several stores in South Africa, which is like a Canadian chain opening stores in the US.

Nearly everyone loved to hate Choppies, but nearly everyone shopped there. My local store was quite small, but within it there were a hot food takeout, an in-store bakery, a section for household goods and dog food, a section for large bags of traditional foods such as cornmeal, a counter that sold cigarettes, toiletries and condoms, and most everything else that you could find in a North American supermarket. There were breakfast cereals such as Special K, instant pudding, baking supplies, instant coffee, tea bags, and a freezer, which among other things displayed frozen French fries and fish sticks. The French fries were of a Canadian brand, McCain, though they were packed in South Africa.

The bakery in Choppies was so-so. Their brown bread was really good when it was fresh and hot. You could buy the bread in one piece and slice it yourself in a special machine at the front of the store, but that machine was much too complex for me. So after ruining two loaves of bread, I decided to buy a loaf that was already sliced or to slice the bread at home with a bread knife I bought from a Chinese household goods store. The bakery also made chocolate-dipped donuts that were not bad, and small whole-wheat phapathas that were quite good. I also liked the little pound cakes, called Madeira cakes that had no icing, so that they were easy to slice and pack for lunch. The bakery's downfall was the display of European-style pastries. There were large colourful cakes with creamy icing that were sold in large slices, but these cakes were inevitably well past their prime, to the point of probably being poisonous.

Like most Botswana supermarkets, Choppies sold takeout hot food, breakfast in the morning, lunch at noon and then whatever was left till the store closed at 8:30 pm. The food was not particularly good — greasy French fries, overcooked spaghetti, the same weird chicken as the cafeteria sold, salty beef stew and so on. Sometimes there was papa and sorghum porridge. There also were salads, somewhat better than those at UB. The salads were kept on a separate cold bar behind the hot food. And all the servers wore hairnets and plastic gloves. Before closing in the evening, any leftover food was sold in small prepacks, which were handy if I wanted to take something home for my dinner.

At lunchtime, there were usually long lines of policemen and construction workers waiting to be served. I don't know why the policemen were there because the refectory for the city police was right across the road. Maybe its food was even worse.

In the summer, Choppies put a soft ice cream machine in front of the store. A small cone, vanilla or strawberry, cost only 3P or $0.42, but I soon learned that that particular indulgence led to a badly upset stomach. I concluded that Choppies did not bother to clean the machine overnight, since soft ice cream elsewhere did not have that effect on me.

The worst part of Choppies was the produce section. Most of what was sold there was either on the point of going bad or was actually mouldy or wilted. Complaints were useless. The attitude of the management was that I should be glad to get anything. I read in a newspaper once that Choppies had been caught trying to resell produce that the government had put into the monthly food baskets given to indigent families. I could believe that.

Outside Choppies in the parking lot, ladies with small tables sold phone cards, matches and cigarettes, though all of that was available in the store. I did buy phone cards from those ladies sometimes, and always bought from them the matches I needed to light my gas stove because I thought that these ladies needed to live too.

Increasingly, dealers selling fresh fruits and vegetables off the back of pickup trucks also set up shop in Choppies' parking lot. After a while, I noticed not only that they paid Choppies for this privilege but that in some cases they were actually selling produce for Choppies. Still what I bought there was of much better quality than what was available in the store. And sometimes there was an extra convenience: Someone selling spinach from the back of a truck would chop it up and sell it in a plastic bag already chopped.

During the three years that I lived in my house, the variety of goods available from Choppies improved greatly. Locally made cheese became available in addition to the sliced ones from South Africa. Sometimes there was butter or bacon. I remember saying that I could buy anything I wanted in the Gaborone supermarkets except parathas (multi-layered flat bread that is a favourite Indian breakfast) and frozen pierogis. Well, the pierogis never did appear but to my delight, in 2012 frozen parathas made an appearance in the freezer at Choppies. They were imported from India but were not expensive and quite tasty.

As Choppies expanded its lines of products, it displayed a very distinctive pricing policy, similar to what I have seen in discount supermarkets in Canada. Ordinary staples were competitively priced, but anything out of the ordinary was expensive. When olive oil appeared at Choppies, for example, it cost exactly double what it did at the mall. I wonder if there are international conventions of supermarket managers where they teach each other these tricks.

One of the nicest aspects of shopping at Choppies was the staff. They got paid a pittance — 600P or $84 a month for a shelver and 900P a month for a cashier. Yet they were nearly always friendly and helpful and ready for a chat. Like most Batswana, they loved receiving little presents. Once on my return from a trip, I brought all the girls little earrings and they were delighted. When I moved out of my house, I gave each of the staff working that morning 20P, and they liked that too, but I think that they were even happier with the earrings.

> *Reality check: To put 600P a month into perspective, I was told that it was possible to rent a room without electricity for 200P per month, a room with electricity for 400P, and a mini-bus fare cost 3.5P each way. I would hope that many of those who worked at Choppies were young people who lived with their families.*

My favourite time at Choppies was Sunday evening. Many people went back to their village or cattlepost (*moraka*) on the weekends. Sunday night nearly everyone was back, ready to go to work on Monday morning, and Choppies was full of people buying supplies for the week: large bags of corn flour or rice, large trays of eggs, bread, milk, tea and breakfast cereals. Since not everyone had electricity, let alone a refrigerator, every supermarket sold ultra-pasteurised long-life milk in boxes. I sometimes bought it too when the fresh milk was too close to the expiry date (I found that Choppies' stuff tended to go bad somewhat before the due date.), and it tasted almost as good as fresh milk. Nearly everyone bought whole milk;

only dieters touched the skim milk. Two percent milk was only available in a few specialty stores.

Of course, Choppies was busiest on the Sunday evening following the last day of the month. The life of Gaborone changes drastically during the last two days and the first two days of the month. This phenomenon is known as "month's end" and is also mentioned in the Alexander McCall Smith novels. Nearly everyone who has a job is paid at the end of the month. (UB paid on the 25th.) Then all the stores and restaurants are busy and full of people, and there are long line-ups in the banks and the electricity and water companies as people come to pay their bills. All the taxi drivers turn up at the ranks in front of the malls, knowing that this was the best time to make money.

The month's end phenomenon demonstrates two characteristics of the culture of everyday life in Gaborone: people spent most of their money during the first week of the month and after that scraped by as best they could, and people also had an amazing tolerance for standing in line. Once when I visited my cell phone company on the 10th of the month, my favourite technician was looking sad. It was her son's fifth birthday, and she had spent all her money for the whole month. There was nothing left to buy him a treat.

As for the line-ups, the line-ups at Botswana Power Corporation were legendary, and when the university library opened in the morning, there must have been a hundred students in line waiting to check their bags and briefcases. And yet never, not even once, did I see a dispute about where in the line someone should be. If you had to leave for a bit, the person behind accepted you when you came back, but at the bank it was not unknown for someone to pay a poor person a few pula to stand in line for her or him.

Just once did someone get impatient in a line. It was in December, before ten in the morning, and already there was a long line at the counter of the electronics store. Only two tills were open. I wanted to buy one adapter and the man behind me with an Afrikaans accent also had only one small item. The Afrikaner got impatient and demanded that the manager open another till. The cashiers, with their bureaucratic Botswana mind-sets, replied that they did not open a third cash until ten. The man's shouting got louder: "Open another cash. It's Christmas. The store is busy." They *did* open another till. Normally I found the loud Afrikaners quite out of place in Botswana, but this one time, I was quite happy to have this man do his thing.

> *Fact check: Houses in Botswana are built with wall receptacles that have either three round prongs, as in South Africa, or three square ones, as in the UK. Most appliances have the South African-type of plug, though some electronic goods have North American-style two-pronged plugs. So there is a high demand for adapters that can connect your gadget with the wall. Of course, the stores always seemed to have exactly the configuration that one did* not *need on that day. Worse yet, each adapter included a little fuse that was irreplaceable and would blow up with a little puff of smoke if one had the misfortune to drop the whole adapter on the floor.*

> *While I lived in the bed-and-breakfast, I had just that misfortune, and it being evening, there was no way of getting another adapter. The lady in the next room was a nurse from Zimbabwe, looking for work in Botswana. She said. "In Zimbabwe we cannot buy anything these days. We learn to make do." She then cut the useless plug off the adapter, extracted the various coloured wires from the cord, and inserted them directly into the wall receptacle — and all of this at 220V. It worked until I bought another adapter.*

Not surprisingly, consumer debt is high in Botswana. I don't know if there are traditional moneylenders; the people I knew just took out bank or consumer loans and paid them back gradually. Credit cards are also becoming common. The political science secretary won a contest at her bank when she applied for a credit card. She won the third prize, a trip to Cape Town with airfare and hotel paid for a week. The second prize was a car with a six months' supply of gas, and the first prize — wait for it — was a bull with four cows. How Botswana!

But to get back to food and the supermarkets: obviously Choppies did not meet all of my needs. Fortunately, there was a shopping mall about twenty minutes' walk from my house. It soon became my favourite mall. Other malls were bigger and glitzier but Riverwalk was of a manageable size. (The river in the name was wishful thinking. It consisted of a wide ditch in which water sometimes flowed during the rainy season.) The mall was built the shape of a +, open at three sides with a supermarket plugging the fourth side of the +. The mall continued to grow toward that side. By the time I left it had spawned a subsidiary mall that included a bank, a second supermarket, various offices, to mention only a few of the businesses, and two novelties, firsts for Gaborone, a flower store and a health food store.

What I liked about Riverwalk was the design which was suitable to a tropical climate. Not only were three sides of the mall open to the outside (albeit an outside consisting of parking lots); the single-storey part of the mall had a slotted roof, something like a picket fence put sideways that provided some shade on sunny days but allowed the rain to pour in too. There were also benches where people could sit and eat takeout food or bounce their little children on their knees or wait for or phone their friends.

At the centre of the +, there was an open space, big enough to put up a stage. And sometimes the mall did just that. There were music and dance performances put on by a local orphanage in the hope that passers-by would donate to their institution when they saw the children in real life. There were similar performances by some of the local private schools. Sometimes there were fashion shows or beauty contests. One weekend before Christmas, there were tables of people asking for donations of toys for poor children. If you bought a toy from the Pick n' Pay supermarket and then donated it, the people at the table gave you a Riverwalk T-shirt. I still have mine.

Increasingly various charities and sometimes businesses set up around the central area, even when there was no stage. I remember a collection for breast cancer victims and one for a planned animal shelter.

I went to Riverwalk mainly for the FOOD. The two supermarkets were a delight. There were bacon, sandwich fixings such as ham, salami, roast chicken slices and liverwurst, fresh produce, including white mushrooms, grapes. strawberries and sometimes cauliflower, cheeses from South Africa, including feta, Camembert, cheddar, Gouda and cream cheese in little tubs (not the bricks that you could use to make cheesecake), in-store bakeries that made various kinds of bread, including a skinny type of baguette and sometimes light rye bread, cakes and lovely little squares, and in the grocery section, tasty blackcurrant jam, a spicy mustard the likes of which I have not found since, those packaged noodles with a creamy sauce that are handy if you are just cooking for yourself, wine vinegar and wonderful olive oil, which I first thought came from South Africa but if you read the fine print came from Spain. The supermarkets also stocked a selection of household goods, toys and South African wine (though the last was not sold on Sundays).

One of the supermarkets, the Pick 'n Pay, had a special section of imported food in the front of the store, breakfast cereals from the US, canned goods from the UK and so on. These were prohibitively expensive; I did not need them; the rest of the store was more than enough to meet my needs. One of my local friends swore that Kellogg's corn flakes were better than the South African brand, but I could not taste any difference.

One little treat I discovered in the Riverwalk supermarkets were South African granola bars, sold under the brand name of Jungle bars. They were delicious, not too sweet; the ones coated in dark chocolate were the best. I took about a dozen home to Canada with me. I shared them with a friend and they were soon gone. When another friend, Tom, was coming to Canada, I asked him to bring some Jungle bars. In Botswana, Tom lived in a small town, and the local supermarket had only one Jungle bar that day. He took it to Montreal and mailed it to me in Toronto, but it never got to me. I do hope that Canada Post enjoyed the Jungle bar.

The Riverwalk supermarkets also had pretty good takeout food. The Spar had a tasty sandwich, dubbed an "executive sandwich". The filling was similar to that of a classic submarine. The Pick 'n Pay had a small salad bar with a variety of salads that I could put into a plastic box and have weighed. With a fresh bun from the bakery, that made a good lunch to take back to my office.

Salad as a food is only gradually gaining acceptance. In the cafeteria at UB, the professors nearly all ate salad, but traditional Batswana men called salad *dijo tsa dipudi* or goat's food. When Syntax and Sarah first came to my house for a meal, Syntax told me categorically that he did not eat salad. One day, when he was driving me to a store at lunchtime and whatever we had come to pick up wasn't ready, we stopped at a Pick 'n Pay for lunch. It was a very hot day, and I filled a little box with nice salads. Syntax looked at me as if I were out of my mind; he had a russian on a bun.

But things changed. In 2012, before I left, I invited Syntax and Sarah over for chilli and a green salad, made by me, with papa made by Sarah. After she and Jason and I had salad, Syntax took what was left in the salad bowl and dumped it all onto his plate. I said, "Syntax, you are eating salad." He mumbled something like, "I do now."

Botswana is probably the only African country without a market. There was no retail food and vegetable market, and no flea market either. There was one mall, a down-market kind of place, where some vendors, mostly women, sold fruits and vegetables outside, sometimes even packaged meats. It was there that I had one memorable Botswana experience. It was hot, and an old lady was selling mandarin oranges for 1P each. I bought one to eat as I walked along and by mistake gave her a 2P instead of a 1P piece. She called after me to come and take my change. This from someone who would consider herself lucky if she took in 20P in a day.

There was one area near the middle of the city called "The Station" because until 2008 there had been a railway station there, and as a consequence many long distance buses still ran from there. In that area, there were a large number of outdoor vendors selling mostly cheap clothing, though some also sold fruits or vegetables. That was the closest Botswana came to having a market.

Well, not quite. At Riverwalk, there was an outdoor craft market for the benefit of tourists and foreigners, on the weekends only. There one could buy all kinds of African trinkets, jewellery, shirts and that kind of thing. And there you needed to bargain. Most of the dealers were Kenyans, not local people.

Gentle reader, you may remember that I wrote earlier that Riverwalk had two and half supermarkets. The half was found inside a South African owned department store called Woolworths, or Woollies for short. This had nothing to do with the five-and-dime store some of my older North American readers may remember. It was a department store modelled on the British chain Marks & Spencer. There you could buy good-quality clothing for a fairly steep price, also a few cosmetics and household goods. About one-quarter of the store was taken up by a grocery section, where there were various kinds of breads imported from South Africa, a frozen food section with frozen ready-made meals, such as lasagne, not otherwise available in Gaborone, an excellent produce section, where I could sometimes buy raspberries and even blueberries, and where cauliflower and celery were always available. Most popular was the dessert section, where there were cakes imported from South Africa, a house brand of yoghurt that was better than what the other supermarkets sold, and little one- or two-serving desserts, such as chocolate mousse or tiramisu. When I felt that I deserved a treat, I would go for one of those desserts.

Everything at Woolworths was considerably more expensive than what one could buy from the other supermarkets, and I preferred the locally made breads to what came from South Africa; even the much-praised Woolworths cakes were not always better than what the local supermarkets produced, and Woolworths cakes cost twice as much. For the most part, I limited my purchases to the occasional dessert or ready-made meal when I had visitors and no time to cook.

The customers at Woolworths were by no means limited to expatriates. Many local people shopped there, especially at the end of the month, and on Saturdays there were such long lines at the grocery till that people went the much less frequented clothing section to pay for their groceries. (Most stores have scanners at the till, as we do in North America.)

I found that as time progressed, I went to Woolworths less often. The local supermarkets increased their choice of offerings, but it was also me. I learned to make do with what the local stores offered. Who needed Woolworths and their line-ups?

> *Reality check: McCall Smith has his fictional heroine Mma Ramotswe do her weekly shopping at the Riverwalk Pick 'n Pay. Of course, that would have been convenient for her because it was just up the road from her husband's auto garage, but I am wondering if she would not also have bought staples from Choppies, where they were less expensive.*

Riverwalk also had the largest single concentration of restaurants anywhere in Gaborone: what is life without eating out? There were about twelve restaurants in Riverwalk, and I had the good fortune to eat in most of them. And as elsewhere, there was some coming and going; for example, someone tried to open a sushi restaurant, but that did not last long in landlocked Botswana where people do not have much of a taste for fishy-tasting food.

The best restaurant in Riverwalk was a locally owned Indian restaurant, founded by a young Sikh born in Botswana. His Indian food was the best I have had anywhere, including India. I did not get to eat there very often because there were no mixed plates. To enjoy at least two different dishes, I needed someone with whom I could share the meal.

Another place with good food was a large and cavernous Italian place, part of a South African chain, but owned by a prominent Motswana entrepreneur in the tourist industry. I avoided this place for some time because it had such garish lighting, bright orange and bright purple. But when I did try it, I found that the food was good and the servings large, even if I ordered the small size. I have several good and/or funny memories of that place. One time a manager came up to me and said, "Why are you eating here by yourself?" I don't remember what I answered.

Another good thing about this restaurant was the internet connection, which was really good, fast and stable. Management encouraged customers to use the internet. They would ask me if my laptop had a round or square plug, so that they could seat me near the appropriate outlet. When Wynie was my housemate, she and I might go there on the weekend with our laptops. We would order a large pasta dish and salad and share both. But we did not do this to enjoy each other's company. We caught up on our email as we ate.

After the very first class I taught at UB, one of my graduate students, Gabriel Malebang, suggested we go out for a meal. He drove me to Riverwalk, and we ate at Nando's. This is a simple fast-food restaurant, a South African-based multinational. They make excellent Portuguese-style barbecued chicken, which has no relation whatsoever to KFC. They have pretty good coleslaw too. The only problem I had with Nando's in Botswana is that they do not serve tea or coffee, only cold drinks. Before long I found out that Nando's is a multinational, with restaurants in Britain, Canada, the US and Australia as well as the countries of southern Africa. To my delight, I have found a Nando's in Toronto not all that far from Glendon College.

My other two regular haunts at Riverwalk were Wimpy's and the place everyone just called "the coffee shop", though its real name was the Equatorial Café. Wimpy's was where I liked to go on Sunday morning for my second breakfast. It is basically a hamburger place, perhaps related to the British chain of the same name, but they also do breakfast. My favourite was a waffle with soft ice cream and chocolate chips accompanied by a latte. I was a faithful customer at Wimpy's until I learned that the coffee shop had free internet, though it was not always working. So I naturally gravitated to the coffee shop, where I learned to ask if the internet was working before I sat down. There I enjoyed a more substantial breakfast, an omelette with three fillings of my choice accompanied by a cup of real filter coffee.

However, giving my loyalty to the coffee shop instead of Wimpy's was not easy. Wimpy's was busy at month's end, but not so busy during the rest of the month, and to go to the coffee shop from elsewhere in the mall, I had to walk by Wimpy's. On more than one occasion, the staff would be standing outside asking me to come in, and ask me why I didn't come any more. I told them that I could do internet at the coffee shop. But, they said, we also have internet. So the next time I came to the mall with my laptop, a manager came and put a password into it, and presto! I was on the internet. But this internet was almost an illusion. It only lasted ten minutes before I had to call the manager to put the password in again.

I have one not-so-pleasant memory of Wimpy's. Once on a weekday, I needed to go to the bank. Walking was not practical. It would have taken about forty minutes each way. I could have called Syntax, but it was awkward for him to take time off on a workday. So I suggested to the two secretaries in our building that one of them could drive, and I would buy lunch for all three of us. Like many Batswana, they liked eating out and readily agreed. I left them in Wimpy's, told them what I wanted to order, and asked them order whatever they liked for themselves while I went to the bank. When I came back, they had sought out the two most expensive items on the menu, lamb chops for one of them and a half grilled chicken for the other. With the tip, the bill came to almost 300p or $40. I was not amused.

That is how I learned that not everyone is Botswana is equally honest and polite. On another occasion, a secretary asked me to create some work for her, so that she could come in on the Saturday and claim overtime. I refused, of course, even though it would not have been my money.

I tried to keep my Sunday mornings slow and easy. I would have a small breakfast of cereal, read newspapers, do a Sudoku and watch television. On Sunday morning until about 10:00, Botswana TV showed a French government news channel, France 24, albeit in English. So I would watch that until I heard a group of schoolchildren singing the Botswana national anthem. That was the signal for local programming to begin. The first program was a religious one, followed by all kinds of local sports. Sometimes I was lazy and was not ready to go to Riverwalk until noon or so when the sun was beating down with full force. Mad dogs and Englishmen as the song goes, and Edelgard I guess, go out in the noonday sun. There was no shade on the walk to Riverwalk. Once in a while people would stop to offer me a lift, and I accepted. Usually they were local people going to shop, but once it was a retired English professor from UB, another time a Bulgarian interior decorator who for some reason had ended up in Botswana; he may have been the only interior decorator in the country.

Anyway, I could not count on getting a lift, and drivers were hard to find on Sundays. Besides, I did not want to call a driver when I could walk. So on one Sunday as the sun beat down and a hat simply would not provide enough protection, I dipped my T-shirt in cold water and put it back on. By the time I got to Riverwalk, I was reasonably cool and the T-shirt was dry. (This was not a wet T-shirt contest of US collegiate fame; I wore a bra under the T-shirt.)

Of course, there were also restaurants in Gaborone beyond Riverwalk. During my first three months in Gaborone, when I was staying in a bed-and-breakfast, there was only one place within walking distance where I could eat in the evenings. It was yet another South African chain restaurant called the News Café, and it was located in an upscale hotel called the Mondior. The food was international fare with a Greek flavour. My favourite dish was a kind of chicken souvlaki with a creamy feta sauce, but there was lots of other standard fare such as sandwiches, pasts, huge salads, steaks and desserts. Unfortunately the News Café changes its menu frequently, so that my favourite dish is no longer available.

Naturally the staff at the café got to know me and showed me to my favourite spot, near the computer plug-in, when I arrived. One day I left my hat in the café. The hat was special because it was of a good Canadian make and it had been a take-to-Africa present from a family friend. When I arrived at the News Café the next evening, four of the waiters and waitresses were standing at the door in a row chanting in unison, "I found your hat." Of course, they wanted a tip. I thanked them for finding the hat and left a generous, more-than-usual tip after my meal.

It was usually daylight when I went to the café; I made sure to walk there during the daylight because I had been told not to walk alone in the dark, but it was always dark by the time I left because in September and October the days are still quite short. To get back to the bed-and-breakfast from the café, I had to call a driver, and since I had not yet built up my own phone list of reliable drivers, I would go to the reception at the hotel and ask someone to call me a cab. That actually was a good way of getting to know reliable drivers. One night when a driver called Kitso picked me up, his car radio was playing a song by Gordon Lightfoot. I said, "That's a Canadian singer." He gave me a weird look as if to say, "Yeah, really."

Beyond the immediate university area, Gaborone had many more restaurants. Batswana like eating out, especially at the end of the month. And anyone who organizes a function is expected to include food, which does wonders for both the restaurant and the catering business. Batswana also have a great talent for getting various aid agencies, private charities and foundations to pony up money for seminars and training sessions of various kinds, which nearly always include some kind of food. To mention only one example: as citizens of one of the not-so-underdeveloped countries of Africa, the people of Botswana laid great stock in making progress toward achieving the World Bank's Millennium Development Goals. One of my University colleagues managed to find funds to organize training sessions at which members of the faculty could learn about the MDGs. Different speakers came in to discuss individual goals. There was, for example, an interesting talk by a gynaecologist/obstetrician about reducing maternal mortality. After several talks, there would be a tea break with sandwiches and cookies and a meal at lunchtime.

Gaborone does not really have a downtown. There is an area called the Main Mall, which is kind of a substitute for a downtown. Adjoining the Main Mall, there is the government enclave (district) with the Parliament buildings and a little bit further away, the President's office. Some of the ministries are located there, though the larger ones, such as the Ministry of Health, are scattered around town. A diplomatic quarter is located a little bit further out, to the West, though several of the embassies, such as the French, EU, South African, Nigerian, Zambian and British, are right downtown. The Americans, though, keep their distance. They and the Scandinavians, Indians, and Chinese are to be found in the diplomatic quarter.

But to return to the theme of food. The Main Mall may have the government offices, main post office, principal branches of the major banks, and the headquarters of Botswana Power, but it has hardly any restaurants. There are three South African chicken and/or hamburger joints and a KFC, two takeout meat pie places, and a couple of small places that serve local food. And there are two discount supermarkets that also serve some food. For people who work downtown the main lunchtime sources of food are vendors who sell hot food from large tubs in the pedestrian area that constitutes the Main Mall. On Thursday through Saturday, vendors selling local souvenirs and locally made leather sandals as well as made-in-China hats, belts, clothes, cell phones and DVDs set up shop there too. During weekday lunch hours they share that space with the food vendors. I never tried their food, but Parkash did and said it was quite good.

There is one restaurant in the Main Mall that claims to serve quality food of the Western variety. Nobantu and I tried lunch there once. It was a disaster. We waited a long time for service, and when we finally got it, it took twenty minutes for the waiter to tell us that they did not have what we wanted, and then they repeated the performance for another twenty minutes. Needless to say we never went back. Recently, Nando's opened a large restaurant at the far end of the Main Mall. It is always busy, as it is walking distance from City Hall and the major national hospital.

Of course, there is also the President Hotel, the one mentioned several times by McCall Smith as a place where Mma Ramotswe liked to go for a tea on the balcony to watch the goings-on in the Mall below. I have no doubt that McCall Smith sometimes enjoyed a cup of tea in that setting. I also did, but I found the coffee shop expensive, even on an ex-pat's salary, and the menu very limited. McCall Smith also has Mma Ramotswe going to the bookstore in the Main Mall, and there was indeed a bookstore there when I first came to Gaborone. By the time I left, the bookstore sold only secondary school textbooks, stationery and magazines. The only real bookstore left was the South African-owned store in Riverwalk, which did have a good selection of books, but never let you forget that its real mission in life was to persuade you to buy Christian fundamentalist literature. The best aspect of that bookstore consisted of a wall of books entitled *Bala Botswana*, literally "Read Botswana". There I found many interesting books about Botswana, books whose existence I had not learned of anywhere else.

I would go to the Main Mall if I wanted to buy an airline ticket directly from the Air Botswana office or an out-of-country bus ticket. Even that was seldom necessary. Most airline tickets I could purchase online, and the offices of other airlines were scattered around the city in various shopping malls.

So much for the restaurant scene in downtown Botswana. Fortunately, there were a number of good restaurants in the rest of the city. The crème de la crème of these was a Portuguese restaurant set among trees in a neighbourhood not too far from downtown and the University. I only ate there once, when the French ambassador invited me to join a group after a function. The food and wine were of high quality, comparable to that in a good restaurant in Toronto.

Off the beaten track, not too far from the main water reservoir for the city, there was, for those who could afford gardening of the leisure kind, rather than gardening to grow food, a nursery that sold garden supplies, and attached to that nursery was an outdoor restaurant that served North American-style brunches. This place could only be reached by car, however, and I wouldn't have paid a driver a fare both ways to an out-of-the-way place to eat brunch.

Scattered around town, in shopping malls, were some other good restaurants: a Portuguese one at the south end of the city and a South African-owned place that served fancy coffees and excellent pasta in the newest and glitziest of the malls (with the unimaginative name of Airport Junction). Tucked away in an industrial area, there was a little square of craft shops that were of interest primarily to foreigners. It included a small Italian restaurant. I only discovered this place during my last week in Gaborone, when my neighbour felt she should do me a favour and drove me there. The life of the Gaborone middle class is almost totally dependent on the use of private cars, and my decision not to buy one did keep me from some places I might have liked to see.

Obviously, there were also restaurants that were not so good; for example, several Indian and one supposedly Thai restaurant that left much to be desired. Missing also was any good Chinese restaurant, which was surprising, considering that Botswana's Chinese population was somewhat larger than its Indian one. One restaurant that we visited specialized in a weird dish that involved a steamed head of lettuce, the leaves of which were to be peeled off and used to scoop up some kind of a goo. In the walled mall called Oriental Plaza there was a hole in the wall that served a greasy version of Cantonese food, which I made sure to have whenever I went there, which was not all that often. Oriental Plaza had been a favourite shopping area where many Batswana could buy household goods and some shoes and clothing at a much lower price than anywhere else in town, but in 2012 the city government decreed that Oriental Plaza was to be limited to wholesale trade. I assume that this had something to do with jealousy from local retailers. In any case, similar Chinese-owned shops soon appeared on the road just outside Oriental Plaza.

Gaborone has one five-star hotel, on the far west side of the city. There the rich can hold weddings, and when someone from the University has enough money to host a well-funded conference, it also usually takes place there. The restaurant offers a magnificent lunchtime buffet, such as one might find in a similar hotel anywhere in the world. Gaborone includes the headquarters of the South African Development Community (SADC) and thus plays host to a number of regional dignitaries. Hence the government decided to allow the construction of a second five-star hotel. The last time I heard, the building was almost ready but no date had been set for the grand opening. Holiday Inn had been a possible franchise sponsor for the hotel but pulled out before the hotel building was finished.

Set amid a pleasant garden is the Cresta Hotel, which includes a conference centre. This hotel restaurant is only affordable if someone else pays the bills, as when there was a reception for the SADC observers of the 2009 Botswana election. In December 2012, a colleague organized a Christmas lunch for some of the lady professors there. We were all supposed to show off our spring hats. I went, but all of us blanched when it came to paying for the lunch. This hotel suffers from another disadvantage. It is located between a car dealership and a nondescript mall and not far from the area called Old Naledi, which is the closest Gaborone comes to having a slum or a township.

My favourite of the local restaurants was the buffet in the Gaborone Sun. This hotel has the great advantage of being within easy walking distance of the University. It has an outdoor pool, a conference centre, a casino and a lobby where dark brown colours predominate, giving an illusion of coolness on even the hottest days. The front desk staff treat everyone with obsequiousness, and there is a hairdressing salon, one of only three in town with hairdressers trained in styling "Caucasian hair" (and for which privilege it charges a pretty penny).

For me the best thing about the Sun was its restaurant. Even for me, who normally does not like buffets, theirs was outstanding, for an outstanding price, of course. At lunch and dinner, the hot food counter was an amazing place, with four stations for Botswana, Indian,

Continental, and Chinese food. At the Chinese food station, one could design one's own stir-fry from a host of ingredients, and the continental station almost always included excellent roast beef. There was also a salad bar, a cheese station and a dessert station with a delicious array of cakes and puddings.

Strangely, the coffee shop in the Sun, which was located around the pool, with some tables in and some outside the building, served food that was not good at all. It offered overpriced dry sandwiches and greasy fish and chips. I could hardly believe that the food came from the same kitchen that produced the buffet.

The Sun had the good sense to offer specials to the locals on holiday weekends, when there were fewer business travellers. From Christmas 2008 to New Year's 2009, Paul, Parkash and I stayed there because there was a special that included dinner as well as breakfast. When it was time for me to leave Gaborone, in December 2012, I persuaded the university's human resources department to let me have three nights — with meals — in the Sun instead of seven in some far-away hotel. It was a treat that made leaving a little less painful.

Two final comments before I leave this section on restaurants and food.

Behind Choppies in my neighbourhood, there was an atypical restaurant. Choppies constituted the bottom of an L-shaped mall. Inside the L, there was the loading and unloading area and the garbage bins from Choppies. On the outside of the L, along the long side, there was a strip mall, and in that strip mall there was a restaurant called the Belgrade. When I first saw it, I thought, great. Here there will be some central European food. But the restaurant served only Botswana food, of a somewhat better quality than could be had at Choppies or the university cafeterias, and for a slightly higher price. The owner was a tall white man of fifty or so, with a long ruddy face and dark hair.

I tried to talk to him and asked him about the name of his restaurant. He said that he was Serbian. The next thought that crossed my mind was: he must be a Serbian war criminal run away far from the court in The Hague. So I asked him how long he had been in Botswana; he became evasive and did not want to talk to me anymore.

In 2012, he changed the name of his restaurant from Belgrade to Ocean Berry, the name of a local soft drink, but he still ran it personally, operating the till at lunchtime. I had little occasion to eat there, but the few times when I did so, I always had good service and big servings. And I still think that the owner might very well be a runaway war criminal. On that intriguing note, we'll leave the subject of food.

WATER — I have mentioned salad several times. Perhaps you, my gentle reader, may have read somewhere not to eat salad in poor countries where it has been washed in water that is not fit to drink. Yes, that may be true of other Third World countries but not Botswana. Over ninety percent of the people have access to clean drinking water. You can drink the water from the tap, just as in Canada. And if any village would have a water problem such that for a few days its water had to be boiled, that made the national news.

Interchapter — The Little Pleasures of Life in Gaborone

- On a Saturday or Sunday morning, walking to the local mall, buying the excellent South African weekly, *The Mail and Guardian*, then across the aisle to Wimpy's restaurant for a waffle with soft ice cream and chocolate sprinkles, accompanied by a latte.
- Seeing a big red sunset behind the trees behind the Alliance française building
- A big wide rainbow over the top of the Riverwalk mall, the widest rainbow I have ever seen
- Perfect strangers or students asking me if they could help me carry my bags
- Standing at the door of my house, watching the rain splash down into the front yard
- Lying in the bathtub, watching the lovely tree in my backyard and listening to the birds
- Flowering trees and shrubs as the rainy season progresses: purple ones, then red ones, and finally clusters of yellow flowers among the leaves

CHAPTER 3   GETTING FROM HERE TO THERE (AND BACK)

Happy as I was to have my very own house, much as I came to enjoy life in Gaborone, I am a mobile thing. I like to get around.

Weather and time of day permitting, I would walk from my house or bed-and-breakfast to the University or the Riverwalk mall or the Alliance française or the Gaborone Sun Hotel or the News Café. Though Gaborone is a city of only 500 000 or so inhabitants, those people and the many shopping malls they frequent are scattered over a large area. Except for the small central government district, town planning is an art that has barely touched this city. My neighbour, an environmental studies professor, had been part of a group that tried to have the city (Gaborone has a city government.) build sidewalks and even bicycle lanes when new streets were paved or laid out, but their lobbying was unsuccessful. There are only a few sidewalks, which may continue for a block or two and then disappear. Indeed, Gaborone hardly has any streets with store fronts or houses in a row. Stores and businesses are mostly found in malls, and houses are grouped together or set back from the road at various angles. If a giant had dropped houses from the sky and let them fall where they may, that might have produced a housing pattern not too different from what one sees in Gaborone.

There are some exceptions. The complex of UB townhouses where I lived had a layout similar to that of the neighbourhoods in Stevenage New Town in Hertfordshire — 1950s British public housing. The housing provided for policeman and military personnel is located in fenced compounds, but the houses are scattered around in the typical Gaborone fashion. Things may be changing, though. The new and upscale suburb of Phakalane has houses strung along real streets. But then who is to say that houses one next to another along a street represent modernity and progress? Maybe Batswana are one step ahead with their post-modern neighbourhoods.

Gaborone's downtown is called the Main Mall, which about describes the inhabitants' attitude toward their city: it consists of malls and houses, not streets. The Main Mall has three parallel streets, each about three blocks in length, anchored by the government district at one end and City Hall, the National Museum and the country's major hospital at the other, but that is almost it for regular streets.

Before I leave the subject of town planning and the lack thereof and turn to the subject of getting around this hodgepodge of a city, I must mention one anomaly. Down the road from the bed-and-breakfast, there was a small park with a children's playground, though I never saw any children play there; the pavement on the street that runs by that park is traversed by a large protuberance, almost a foot wide, several inches high and neatly rounded on top. At first I thought that this was just the reverse of the many potholes that appear after the rainy season, but then I realized that this was Gaborone's attempt at traffic calming. That waste of taxpayers' money, putting bumps onto perfectly good roads, has found its way to Botswana.

That bump in the road is hugely symbolic. It encapsulates the Batswana attitude to modernity: If they have it, we should copy it. Another example is the concept of civil society. Theorists of democracy have for centuries, at least since Alexandre de Tocqueville, pointed out that voluntary organizations constitute useful building blocks and training grounds for a democratic government. If Botswana wants to be democratic, it needs civil society. The government has set up an office where nationwide civic groups can register and receive govern-ment assistance. This, for example, is the case of groups advocating for the rights of women and of the national organization promoting the observance of human rights.

Back to Gaborone and its non-streets. Though there are streets of a sort, there are no street addresses, and no mail delivery either. If you are not lucky enough to have a work address, you must pick up your mail from the post office. Still, occasionally it is necessary to find a precise address. The Botswana Power Authority needs to find your house to read the electricity meter, ditto for the Water Utilities

Corporation. The police must know where to go should you be unlucky enough to have a break-in, and likewise the security companies should you wish to install a security system to prevent such a break-in.

For this purpose there are plot and house numbers. The city is divided into chunks of land called plots, each one containing as many as a hundred houses, and each house has an individual number. To the best of my knowledge, there is no map of plots with their corresponding numbers; perhaps the city has one, but if so it does not share it with anyone. And the plot numbers do not follow any logical sequence, say from north to south. Since there appears to be no logical sequence, I assume that they were numbered as they were built. (There are a few touristy maps of Gaborone, but they are short on details.)

People who have lived in Gaborone for a long time usually know their way around, as do those, like cab drivers, whose jobs require them to have that information. The rest of us needed to rely on friends or professional drivers.

I decided early on that I would not buy a car. To begin, Botswana drives on the left. For another, most cars have a manual transmission, though automatic was becoming more common by the time I left. Worst of all, there are plenty of bad drivers, and drunk driving is a big problem, though the government has taken many measures to try and stamp it out. I remember a university party at a restaurant. A colleague from India offered me a lift home. I could see that he had had a fair amount to drink, so I said no, someone was already driving me. My friend Dorothy from my department drove me home. It was a Friday night, and there were many cars weaving all over the road. Botswana has a high percentage of car ownership for a developing country. There are two-thirds as many passenger cars as people. That number includes cars owned by businesses and the government, but it still makes for many cars. Not surprisingly, the death toll from traffic accidents is also high; according to the WHO it was 401 in 2011. Another good reason not to do my own driving.

So what were the alternatives? There is no government-supported public transit in Gaborone. Public transit consists of a thousand or so combis, which are similar to the minibuses of Hong Kong, except that to compare Hong Kong minibuses to Gaborone combis is like comparing a Rolls Royce to a second-hand Chevrolet. Hong Kong minibuses are neat and clean and have exactly sixteen seats. There is a centre aisle, so that there is a minimum of crawling over other passengers. Gaborone combis have just one aisle, on the left-hand side. There is one long seat in the back, and three somewhat shorter rows of seats in front of that one. But since there is only one aisle on one side, getting in or out means climbing over the other passengers or — and this is the more common solution — everyone else has to get out and climb in again if say the last passenger in the rear seat needs to leave. I tried a few times to explain that it might make sense to have the people who were getting off last to sit in the back, but this logic did not appeal to anyone I spoke to. People climbed in and out in the order in which they had got in.

Once, just once, I tried to get out of a combi at UB and a rather fat teenage boy sitting next to me refused to move. This was most uncharacteristic as I was usually treated with a lot of respect. But this incident had a bad consequence. When I climbed over the lout, my phone fell out of my pocket, never to be seen again, at least by me.

I must say that people were wonderfully helpful and sympathetic when the tragedy of the lost phone struck. I mean, a Motswana is totally lost without his or her phone. The country has about 30% more cell phones than people. My friend Nobantu, who happened to be stopping by my office, lent me her phone for the afternoon, so that I could make calls and try to recover my phone or make arrangements to get another one. Syntax, my regular driver, drove me to Riverwalk, where I found the South African-owned cell phone company to be most efficient. The staff were able to determine that my phone had not yet been used since its disappearance. They blocked its number and assigned it, my former number, to a new phone, which I had to buy. They were also able to transfer all the credit (*airtime* in Botswana parlance) that I had on the old phone to the new one. So all I had to spend was 200P for a new phone, and all the thief had left was a cheap phone with a disabled number and no airtime. My great regret was losing all the numbers I had stored in the stolen phone.

Most of my combi rides were uneventful if less than comfortable. Each combi held seventeen people, and at rush hour they were full. Except for babes in arms and children small enough to sit on a lap, that total was never exceeded. The police kept a careful eye on combis and often stopped them to inspect papers. There was no packing the vehicle as would have happened in India. There was one exception to the passenger limit. During the afternoon rush hour, the driver was sometimes accompanied by a sidekick who collected the fares. Since the combis were always packed at rush hour, the sidekick squeezed into the combi sideways, his back against the sliding door, his legs akimbo along the side of the combi, until he resembled a flat figure from a wooden jigsaw puzzle.

When there was no sidekick, the driver collected the fares by extending his arm backwards across the second row of seats towards the door, his hand curled into an open cup. A long arm was clearly a qualification for becoming a successful combi driver.

The inside of the combi was usually in pretty rough shape; the plastic seats might be torn, disgorging what was left of the upholstery stuffing, or worse, the hinges on the seats might be damaged, causing the seat to tilt forward and tossing the passenger onto the floor when the vehicle passed over a bump or through a pothole.

All combis had bench seats in the front, long enough for the driver and two passengers. These two seats were the driver's gift. It was a privilege to be asked to sit there, since that meant no one would be climbing over you or force you to get out while they descended. The drivers usually asked pretty young girls to sit next to them, or failing that, their buddies, but once in a while a driver asked me to sit in the front. This involved climbing up from the pavement over the front wheel and down again when I got out, but I would never have turned down the honour. Of course there were no seatbelts; so those front seats were also the most dangerous. Seatbelts are mandatory for the driver and anyone sitting in the front seat of passenger cars, and there are hefty fines for not wearing them. But I never saw a seatbelt in a combi.

The interiors of the combis may have been in rough shape, but they ran well enough. Only once did a combi break down with me inside. I had taken one to the discount mall the name of which is Kagiso (peace), but which everyone calls BBS after an office building found there. About two-thirds of the way there, the engine sputtered and the combi stopped. Fortunately we were at the side of the road. I thought, great; now it will be hours before I get to the mall. But no. The driver made some calls, and in about ten minutes another combi appeared and we were on our way again — without having to pay a second fare.

Almost all the passengers in the combis were locals or perhaps Zimbabwean immigrants. I did not see another white person in a combi, though once there was someone who might have been white or an African albino. Once or twice I saw a Chinese person, and on one occasion an East Indian woman with two children. In the combis, then, I was quite a sight. Little kids would stare at me. I got into the habit of carrying individually wrapped candies in my purse, so that I could give them to the children. I hoped that this would give them a good impression of my race. I did not, however, interact with the hordes of school children in their uniforms, some of them no more than eight or nine years old, who took the combis after school.

> *A note about vocabulary: Local people frequently refer to others by their race; whites especially were often singled out for that designation. That grated on me. Referring to persons by their race makes me think of apartheid and separate facilities in the American south and all that. But sometimes when you are in Rome... In order to relate to the local people, I at least had to try to understand the way they think and see their world, which meant sometimes reverting to their vocabulary. A relevant incident: One morning, Syntax was driving me to the University, and the gate leading to the Social Science building was closed. Syntax asked the security guard to open it, saying he was just driving in to drop a* lekgoa,

a white person. Of course, Syntax didn't think that I had understood. When we were past the guard, I got angry at Syntax, telling him that I did not want to be referred to in that way. Syntax sensed that he had done something wrong and apologized profusely, saying that he did not think I would understand.

Combi drivers have a reputation for rudeness, and some of them lived up to that reputation. But many were just regular people, polite and even kind. Once when I had to change combis at "the station", the place where there used to be a railway station and where most of the combis turn around at some point during their run, the driver got out and walked me over to my next combi stop to show me where it was.

Combis are driver-owned, but their routes are set by the city council, and the government sets the fare, which is 3.5P or about 50¢. There is no such thing as a transfer. If your trip requires two combis, you pay two fares. That can be a real hardship for a supermarket shelver who makes 600P a month. Two combis each way means 14P a day. In fact, maids charge extra if they have to take two combis to your house.

Which brings me to another problem with the combis. The routes were laid out a long time ago, before many of the malls, buildings, private colleges and so on were built, and it seems impossible to change the routes. It as if they were divinely ordained. The University, for example, is about half an hour's walk from the Riverwalk mall, and Riverwalk with its pubs and restaurants and supermarkets is very popular with students and staff, but to get there you need to take two combis by a roundabout route. A direct combi would be full all the time, but that just does not seem to be possible.

Another problem with the combis is that they only run from six in the morning until about 8:30 pm, which makes life difficult for students who have an evening class or people who work in restaurants. Also, because the combi drivers drive when they feel like it, they tend to be in short supply on holidays, especially long weekends, when the drivers go home to their villages. On New Year's Day 2009 I had gone to my office to check email. Later I came out to catch a combi home, with my laptop case in my hand (later I learned to disguise the laptop by putting it into my backpack or throwing it into a canvas shopping bag). I found a number of students waiting but no combis in sight. Finally a combi came, but it was full. Right behind it there was a police van, and the police chose this occasion to check the combi driver's license and other papers. So no one dared overfill the combi.

The combi left, but the police stayed. No other combi appeared, and it was getting dark. I went over to the police and asked if they could find me a cab. All of my regular drivers had gone home to their villages, and there was no cab in sight either. The policeman who drove the van made a couple of phone calls, but had no more luck than I did. (There were two policemen and a policewoman in the van. Gaborone has numerous female police officers.) I appealed to their prejudices, saying that it was not safe for me to stand there with my laptop when it was getting dark. They asked me where I was going, and I told them to the Village, a neighbourhood near the Choppies supermarket (which happened to be right across the street from the police cafeteria that served police from the whole city). They explained that they were not allowed to drive off their route, but that they could drive me to Choppies. It turned out that the back of the van was equipped for carrying prisoners, and I climbed in. It was my first ride in a paddy wagon. Will it be my last?

When I think back to the time I spent in combis, I try to think less of the torn upholstery and the tilting seats and the constant in and out or the fat teenager over whom I had to climb the day I lost my phone; instead I try think of the times when the combi came together and erupted into a common discussion, be it about a football game or a fare increase (At one time, it was actually a decrease.) mandated by the government. I could not understand the details of what my fellow passengers were saying, but I could grasp the subject matter. And it was a wonderful feeling to be at least on the margin of the local community.

I was hoping to include a picture of a combi with this chapter, but the pictures just show a van, no different from a Hong Kong minibus. Photos do not catch the scratches in the exterior paint, the torn upholstery, the sagging seats. Some things just have to be left to the imagination.

Besides combis, there were two other means of public transit in Gaborone: taxis and cabs, and they were not the same thing. Taxis are mini-combis, whereas cabs are individually owned cars that operate from fixed stations. Taxis were small cars that could just squeeze three people into the back and one next to the driver in the front. They have a sign on top that says taxi. They charge a fixed fare of 5P within the city, as long as you stay on the route which the previous passengers had selected. I was never able to figure this out because some taxis also appeared to have fixed routes. For example, in the afternoon a number of them ran from the University to the station, so that students who lived in the suburbs or nearby villages could connect with the appropriate combis. Other taxis ran to a mall with the peculiar name of African Mall, and still others to the meteorology station down the road from the police cafeteria. But they did *not* run where they would have been most useful: from the University to Riverwalk.

If there were no other passengers, it was possible to ask a taxi to take you wherever you wanted to go, like your own house, but then the fare quintupled to 25P. Of course, the taxi drivers liked the idea of such trips. Whenever I asked one to drive me to a specific place, he would utter the magic word "Special" that unlocked the 25P fare.

One more little fact about taxis; all of the combi and cab drivers I encountered were men, but Gaborone did have one taxi driver who was a woman.

Given their unpredictable routes, I did not use the taxis very often. Instead, I relied on cabs. These had their own traditions and rules. Like the taxis and combis, they were owner-driven, but they had no distinguishing marks and looked just like regular family cars. There were two ways to catch a cab: you could phone the driver or you could go to a cab station and take your chance on the first driver in line. Since Syntax was a cab driver in addition to his day job at the University, I learned quite a bit about the cab business.

Cabs were allowed to solicit business from fixed stations in the malls and in front of hotels. The drivers had their own unwritten rules as to who could join them. If a new driver tried to solicit business at an established station, the waiting drivers would warn him off, and if that did not work, they might threaten to beat him up to make the point.

There were two cab stations at Riverwalk, one near the shopping area and the other near the pubs and restaurants. Syntax was stationed at the more lucrative restaurant end of the mall; my other driver, Robert, was at the shopping end. There business tended to peter out after 7:00 pm on weekdays or 5:00 on Saturdays, when all the shops except the supermarkets closed. Of course, the shopping side drivers were sometimes tempted to try and solicit business on the restaurant side, but they would be chased away if they tried to do so. For a while I had a driver, Kitso, a big, tall, dark Kalanga guy with two teeth missing, who was stationed on the shopping side; Syntax complained that sometimes Kitso would appear on the other side, and then Syntax and his driver friends would have to "chase" him.

The same rules applied all over the city. Syntax lived near the Gaborone Sun Hotel and he once tried to get the drivers there to allow him to have a spot, but he was chased away, just as his group had chased Kitso. Syntax was quite upset at being treated in this way and did not tell me or Sarah what had happened until we noticed that he was so glum. But them were the rules....

Another rule was that the drivers took the business in the order in which it arrived, but the customer always had the right to ask for a specific driver. If a driver left in response to a phone call from a customer, he would lose his place in line and would have to go to the end. Once when I phoned Syntax to drive me from UB, he refused and sent someone else because he had been in line for a long time and was hoping to catch a long-distance customer. But normally, as soon as I came out of Riverwalk, the drivers would start calling for Syntax. If he was not there, I would ask for Modise or Daniel, two of Syntax's friends who would take me home safely and not overcharge me. It was similar on the shopping side; the drivers knew that I was Robert's customer. Sometimes they would tease me and tell me that Robert was not there, even though I could see his car in front of me.

One annoying aspect of this system was that there were no cabs at the side and back of the mall. If I went to the supermarket that was located to one side, I either had to drag my groceries around the side of the mall and down six or seven steps to the cab station or roll my shopping buggy right around the parking lot to avoid the steps, neither of which I was inclined to do on a hot day. So I would phone Syntax or Robert to come for me. Although the cabs were unmarked and to me were undistinguishable from any other car, the mall security knew who they were, and as soon as Syntax came to pick me up, a red-coated security guard would appear and start yelling at him in Setswana. Syntax ignored him, but I might shout back, "Can't you see that I have groceries to carry?" But once, when I had called Robert and the red-coated guard appeared, Robert passed him a 5P coin, and the red monster calmed down right away.

Another aspect of the cabs was that you paid whatever you could negotiate. I learned that my American acquaintances paid more than I, a regular customer, paid, but my local colleagues or students who occasionally needed a cab paid even less than I did. That's just the way it was, and there was little I could do about it. If I mentioned the lower local rates to Syntax, he just smiled mysteriously.

Finding a cab on a Sunday could be a problem. Syntax coached his football team all day long; Robert went home to his village near Mochudi to visit his mother and brother; Modise went to church, one of those long fundamentalist services that lasted most of the day. By the time the stores had closed, after 2:00 pm, there might be no drivers left at either station. Yet I liked to do my shopping, buy the excellent South African paper, the *Mail and Guardian*, and then settle down at one of the restaurants with a latte or an iced coffee, depending on the season, by which time it might be close to 3:00 pm.

One Sunday there were no drivers to be found. Finally an irregular emerged from the corner by the electronics store where they lurked while trying not to attract the attention of the regular drivers. I got into his car, sitting in the front seat as I usually did until then, to show that I was a regular person, not some kind of foreign snob. The drive from Riverwalk to my house was not long. I could walk it in twenty minutes. When we were about halfway home, he put his hand on my arm and started stroking me. He said, "I will give you my phone number. You will call me again, won't you?" all the while still stroking my arm. So I said, "Let go, so that I can take your phone number." I took it, and by that time we were home. I never called him, of course, and I did not again get into the front seat with drivers whom I did not know.

One another occasion, while my husband was visiting, we went out for a meal at Riverwalk, and it was late and dark when we were ready to go home. We went to the cab station, but none of my regular drivers were there. The next in line was another Daniel, not the one who was Syntax's friend. We told him that my house was near the Village Choppies. Remember that there are no street addresses in Gaborone. It did not take me long to figure out that we were not going the right way. Soon I saw a Choppies, but not the one near my house. I had a vision of the guy robbing us and dropping us in the pitch dark by the side of the road. I had to do some quick thinking. First I told him that this was not the right Choppies. I continued by telling him that I knew most of the drivers at Riverwalk and that several of them were friends of mine. I started listing the names, Syntax, Modise, Daniel... I figured that if he harmed us, the others would chase him from his lucrative spot at the restaurant/pub side of Riverwalk. It worked! He apologized, said that he had taken us to the wrong Choppies by mistake, and he took us home. Later, I told Syntax what had happened, and he said that that was a bad guy and that I should never go with him again. Why didn't he tell me that before? And if the other drivers knew that this one was a bad one, why did they tolerate him in their midst?

Just as journalists take shortcuts by interviewing taxi drivers, my drivers gave me a glimpse into local life. I learned that a good driver who knew his way around and spoke and understood a reasonable amount of English was a huge asset anywhere in southern Africa. Robert was the exception that proved the rule. He spoke hardly any English, and I had to speak very slowly to communicate with him. He was single and was able to save money, so that by the time I left he had got rid of his original blue jalopy, replaced it with a nice car, and then replaced the car with a six-seater similar to Syntax's, but even nicer with fancy soft white upholstery. He told me that he would sell that nice car and buy himself a bakkie (small pickup truck) and go back to his village and start a chicken farm. Last time I heard he was still driving. I think that there are thousands of people all over the world who talk about going back to their village but stay on in the city. City life is so much better, isn't it?

> *Reality check: The hundreds of cars that become cabs or that temporary expatriates or ordinary Batswana drive, are second-hand cars from Japan and Singapore The exporters remove the catalytic converters and anything that might make the cars cleaner but more expensive to drive and ship them to South Africa's port of Durban. From there they are brought to Botswana on large car-carrying trucks and end up at a few dealerships on the outskirts of Gaborone. Only wealthy or well-paid people buy the new Volkswagens, Mercedes, BMWs and Audis that are available in town.*
>
> *While I was in Botswana, the South African government announced that it would levy a sizeable transfer tax on the cars that landed at Durban but were shipped on to another country. They cited the cost of maintaining their roads, which made some sense. A howl of protest went up from nearly everyone in Botswana from the government down. Within a month the government of Botswana announced that it was negotiating with Namibia to have cars brought in through Walvis Bay. The South African*

government reduced the amount of the levy, and that was the end of that, but, the negotiations with Namibia are ongoing. The two governments are planning to build a railway from Walvis Bay to northern Botswana, primarily to export Botswana minerals, but if that railway is ever built, the trains could carry imports to Botswana on their return from Walvis Bay.

In Lüderitz in southern Namibia, my driver was David, who was actually an employee of the hotel. He told me lots of stories about his family, how he had for a long time been the only one with a steady job, but when his brother got a job, the brother wouldn't help out, and he, David, supported his sister, so that she could go to university, but she got pregnant and chose not to go to work. Now that could have happened almost anywhere in the world.

When we went to Zambia to see Victoria Falls, we found a driver called Chris among those who hung around the hotel. He not only was good and knowledgeable, but also, when Parkash left his wallet on the tour boat after we had gone on a sunset cruise on the Zambezi, Chris drove him right over to the office of the tour company, and, amazingly, Parkash got his wallet back with both credit cards and cash inside.

The best driver of all — after Syntax — was Selepe, a Setswana-speaking taxi driver who was stationed at the beautiful Protea Hotel Balalaika in Sandton, a wealthy suburb of Johannesburg. When he was not driving, Selepe spent all his time reading about South Africa so that he could give knowledgeable tours. For example, he told us that it was a good idea to visit the Museum of Afrikaner History before visiting the Apartheid Museum because that way one could understand the mentality that led to apartheid. Unfortunately, by that time we had already done our touring the other way around. When South African Express — an airline that specializes in losing and damaging luggage — lost one of our suitcases, Selepe took me to the airport and helped me look for it. Eventually I found it in the Air Botswana storage, where the nice staff allowed me to retrieve it and stayed a few minutes past closing time to help me. Selepe charged me only for the trip, not for the waiting and helping time.

I relied on Selepe whenever I visited Johannesburg, but unfortunately he is no longer driving a cab. He made a ton of money (his expression) during the 2010 World Cup soccer tournament, then realized that with the new overhead train, the Gautrain, that runs from the airport to Sandton and beyond, there would be less taxi business. So he sold his beautiful blue Mercedes and bought a combi, which he drives somewhere in Johannesburg. I still call Selepe whenever I go to Johannesburg, and he finds me a driver who is honest and reliable.

When Parkash and I visited Johannesburg on the Easter weekend in 2012, Selepe sent a driver called Mike to pick us up from the bus station. I needed a new charger for my Acer laptop, and we asked Mike to take us to a computer shop. It was Thursday before the weekend. Mike took us to an Apple store. I told him that this was the wrong store. He protested that this was a computer store. I told him, "Yes, but you wouldn't take a Ford to a Toyota garage." I insisted that he take us to the Sandton City Mall, where I knew that there was an electronics store. The store did not have the charger and the staff gave us the address of the Acer distributor. The clock was ticking. The Acer place was 4km away, and it was the beginning of a long weekend. We got there just a few minutes before 4:30 pm, and the Acer staff were very helpful; they found me a charger and installed it and let me pay for it with my Botswana debit card. And Mike charged us a reasonable price for the whole afternoon of driving.

Intercity travel

Most of the people I knew in Gaborone flew when they wanted to go to South Africa. When I first came to Botswana, the only foreign flights from Gaborone were those to Johannesburg, so that when Paul and I went to Namibia we had to fly to Jo'burg and then to Windhoek, which was definitely a long way around and expensive. Ditto when Parkash and I went to Livingstone in Zambia to see Victoria Falls. But things have changed. In 2010 Kenya Airways started flying from Gaborone to Nairobi. And by 2012 there also were flights to Windhoek and Lusaka two or three times a week. But to go overseas most people still went to Johannesburg. It has a lovely airport with many beautiful shops. I actually like spending time there. And to go to other places in South Africa, such as Cape Town or Durban, it was in any case necessary to pass through Jo'burg.

In February 2009 the undergraduate students at UB went on strike after the government cut their maintenance allowances, which had been quite generous. No settlement of the strike seemed in sight. I decided to take the opportunity to spend a few days in Cape Town. I booked a flight through a South African travel agency someone had recommended to me. At that time, I did not yet know how easy it was to do these things myself by just going to the office of the appropriate airline. The travel agency booked me on South African Express, and on the morning of the flight, South African Express sent me an SMS (text message) to confirm my flight. Syntax drove me to the airport.

When I arrived, the lady at the check-in counter asked me for my credit card. I whipped out my Visa card. She said that that was not the right card. She wanted to see the card that was used to book the flight — but that card belonged to a South African travel agent and was not available to me at 7:00 am. I offered to pay for the ticket a second time with my credit card, but she refused to take my money. And she kept this up until the flight had left and I had thus missed the connection to Cape Town. After the travel agency opened in South Africa, the travel agent faxed a copy of his credit card, and I was able to board the 11:00 am flight. But when I arrived in Johannesburg to transfer to a flight to Cape Town, there was a thunderstorm, and the flight was delayed. So I did not get into Cape Town till evening and lost a whole day of my three-day trip.

I was furious. How could that woman refuse to let me board when I offered to pay for the ticket a second time, taking my chances on getting the money back from the travel agent? I asked the South African Express office in Gaborone to refund me the cost of a one-way ticket to Jo'burg. At first they ignored me. When I persisted, I got promises of action, but no action. After a couple of months, I sent an email to the head of customer relations in Johannesburg. She wrote back to say that she sympathized, but that any action was up to the office in Gaborone. But she must have done *something* because, before too long, the local manager himself appeared in my UB office. (His wife was a professor at UB. The Botswana middle class is small; people are connected and know one another.) The manager promised to do "something", but nothing happened, and after that he did not return phone calls — again.

By the beginning of August, six months after the original incident, I had had enough. I wrote an email to the consumer columnist at one of the local papers, the *Mmegi*. The columnist did not reply to my email, but the next week the manager of South African Express appeared in my UB office again, this time with a promise of a free ticket to Jo'burg. Within two weeks his son, a student at UB, brought me an envelope which included a voucher for a ticket to Johannesburg, minus the taxes. Persistence had paid off.

With one exception, most of the rest of my travels throughout southern Africa were unadventurous. I made a quick trip to Mauritius in January 2009. I found Air Mauritius to be less professional than any of the other African airlines I dealt with. The flight from Mauritius back to Johannesburg departed seven hours late — without any explanation. The tourist hotel in which I was staying had the nerve to tell me that I could stay on for lunch for the modest price of $60. I refused of course and used the time to take a tour of the capital, St. Louis, with a taxi driver I met through a Canadian contact. With hindsight, I think that perhaps the whole thing was a put-up job between the hotels and the airline.

In October 2012, when the University had its short break — we call it study week in Canada — everyone I knew was too busy or too broke to go anywhere with me. So I decided to go to Lüderitz in southern Namibia by myself. The travel brochures made it sound quite alluring: a quiet resort on the south Atlantic, with many historical sites from the time of German colonialism (1888–1916).

I did not find Lüderitz all that alluring. I had a large hotel room with a view of the Atlantic Ocean, the food in the hotel was good, and the staff extremely helpful. But there were drawbacks. The historical sites were only open when there were groups of tourists to see them. I was lucky in that I was able to see the ghost town, a mining town which had been abandoned during the 1920s, because there was a group of North American motorcyclists touring Africa, heading north from South Africa, and Lüderitz was one of their first stops. They went to see the ghost down, and I was able to tag along. There were two couples from Canada in the group. The one I spoke to consisted of a middle-aged man with an Oriental-looking wife, possibly a mail-order bride. She complained of the heat and did not seem keen on this project of riding up the coast of Africa through the Kalahari Desert on the back of a motorcycle.

Another drawback of Lüderitz was that there were no taxis or combis, so that I was completely dependent on the transport provided by the hotel. Walking was not too successful either. The town was spread out, and when I stopped in a small grocery store to ask for directions, the staff were shocked and asked how the hotel could allow me to wander around like that. Another drawback of walking was that the streets were dusty and unpaved. Also, when I tried to find a local restaurant other than the dining room in the hotel, I learned that almost everything closed on Saturday afternoon. And on Sunday morning the hot water at the hotel conked out. It could not be fixed until late on Sunday because the only local plumber, we were told, was suffering from a hangover.

> *For North is North, and South is South*
> *And ever the twain shall meet*
> *Though we may not ever stand in front of God's judgement seat.*
> *But there is neither North nor South nor East nor West*
> *When two good women work side by side*
> *Though they come from the ends of the earth.*
>   (with apologies to Rudyard Kipling)

Comment – Kipling found the ends of the earth in British India where it faded off into Afghanistan. I can think of only two places that I have visited and that would qualify: one is Lüderitz. The other is Uranium City in northern Saskatchewan where I worked during the summer of 1961. There was no radio contact with the outside world; no roads; newspapers came in three days late. The only contact with the outside world was by propeller plane twice a week and by barges which brought in supplies during the summer months, when the rivers and lakes were not frozen. I preferred the Lüderitz end of the earth.

Reaching Lüderitz had not been easy. The only way to fly there was to fly to Johannesburg, then to Windhoek and from there down to Lüderitz, which was really a very long way around, south, then north and then south again. I decided to save money by taking the "bus" from Gaborone to Windhoek and flying from there. The Political Science secretary did that twice a year. I had taken the bus to Johannesburg, and it was quite comfortable, just like a Greyhound bus in North America. But when Syntax took me to the station, the bus turned out to be a large and well maintained combi, something like the minibuses that hotels in North America use to take people to the airport. Because Syntax and I had been looking for a bus, I was one of the last to get on this combi, and I had to share a seat with a young lady. Now the sitting part of this lady's body was about the same size as mine, and we did not fit onto the seat. Whoever sat on the outside kept sliding off onto the floor.

> *Aside: Traditionally among Batswana, a large behind was considered an attractive feature for women.*
>
> *At the cultural village south of Gaborone, the guides told us that young men used to choose their wives by watching a group of ladies dressed in loincloths dance around a fire. The girls would dance with their faces to the fire, and the young men would form a larger circle, so that they could have a good look at the buttocks and choose the most attractive ones. The fact is that, be it by natural selection or otherwise, a large number, perhaps one-third or one-quarter of the local women do have large hips and buttocks; even some little girls have that feature.*

Apart from the problem of the seat that was too small for two ladies of traditional stature, we had a smooth ride to the border, stopping at a couple of clean and well-equipped roadside stops. The border crossing was not nearly as busy as the one on the South African border. A pair of Botswana officials stamped our passports, and that was about it. But then something strange happened. We were not allowed to get back into the bus. There was no food or water available, not even seats. Fortunately, the weather was good, and we twenty or so passengers (including a German woman and some young people from the Netherlands) sat on a stone fence. As I had come brought some food and water with me, I was not too uncomfortable.

After about an hour and a half, the Botswana border guards emerged from the small customs shed and ordered us to pull our luggage off the luggage trailer. They examined it, but did not search it very thoroughly.

Finally, we were told that the reason for the delay was that the Botswana border officials had detained one passenger. The driver called the headquarters of his company and was told to proceed without the passenger of interest. We got back in and continued on our way. Now we were one passenger less, and my former seatmate used the opportunity to take the spare seat, leaving me to continue the journey in some comfort.

There were no more rest stops on the way to Windhoek, but we were two hours behind schedule. When some passengers said they needed to relieve themselves, the driver stopped by a dark, empty field. Fortunately, I did not need that facility. When we arrived in Windhoek in the dark, I was lucky to find a taxi to take me to the hotel. The next morning I flew to Lüderitz in one of the thrice-weekly flights from Windhoek. It was Saturday, and there would be no return flights until Tuesday.

As I said, Lüderitz was not very exciting, and though I had brought some research work with me — as the snail carries his house, I like to carry some work with me — by Sunday I thought that I had seen everything I was likely to see. The hotel was comfortable enough, and I should have stayed in my nice room with its view of the ocean.

But that Sunday I went for a drive to the supermarket with David, the hotel driver who had been sent to buy groceries for the evening meal. I went to the supermarket because supermarkets are interesting places that tell you a lot about local life. I learned that Lüderitz was quite isolated. Only Namibian newspapers were available, nothing else, not even papers from South Africa. The newspapers were in English and Afrikaans; there was also one in German.

And there, on the dusty main street of Lüderitz, I saw a combi. Since there is no local transport in Lüderitz, I asked David what the combi was doing there. "Oh," he said, "there is a combi once a day to Windhoek."

So I was not faced with the choice of a thrice-weekly flight to Windhoek or once-a-week bus to South Africa. There was another way out. I said that I wanted to take the combi the next morning. David, of course, tried to talk me out of it. He even found one of the managers of the hotel to try and talk me out of it. But I was determined, and not so much because I was so uncomfortable or bored in Lüderitz. I had, after all, brought work with me. It was the idea of the combi that fascinated me. If local people could travel 700 km in a combi, why couldn't I?

So the next morning at ten, David brought me and my luggage to the combi stop. David made sure that I got a seat in the second row, just behind the driver. He left and did not even wait for a tip.

It turned out that a Lüderitz combi operates on a schedule like that of a Bulgarian ferry: it leaves only when it is full. So we sat in that combi for about an hour before it finally left. And the combi was not the comfortable minibus that I had taken from Gaborone to Windhoek. It was just like one of the combis that cruise around Gaborone, i.e. torn upholstery, sagging seats and all.

I was lucky in a way. Most of the passengers were Pentecostal church people travelling to a convention in Windhoek, a group who were not rough or rowdy. I was hoping that they might sing some hymns, but they did not. I was sitting between a well-dressed middle-aged woman who must have been some kind of leader in the church — she was reading a book on how to be a leader — and a young man she called her son, but who turned out to be a kind of protégé she was inducting into the church. They had packed food that they passed back and forth to each other across my lap. They spoke to each other in English, meaning that they probably had different tribal backgrounds.

> *A note about languages in Namibia: Namibia's people speak fourteen different languages, including English and Afrikaans. English is the only official language, but in Lüderitz, Afrikaans appeared to be the lingua franca. I noticed that even local Africans often spoke Afrikaans to each other.*

The road to Windhoek was paved and in excellent condition. At one point I saw some horses in the distance to the east of the road. I wondered if they were the famous wild horses of Lüderitz. Horses are not native to Africa, and these horses seem to have adapted to the climate — Namibia is the driest country in the world — by living on less water than European horses need. They are also smaller than European horses. No one knows where these animals came from; the best guess I heard was that their ancestors might have escaped from a wrecked Portuguese ship.

We stopped twice at roadside rest stops; these were clean and well equipped. As one included a Wimpy's, I was able to eat familiar food. The other just sold sandwiches. By the late afternoon, we were seriously behind schedule, and the driver started pushing it, though he did agree to make one more rest stop at a gas station when a passenger asked for a bathroom break. This gave the rest of us a chance to get out and stretch our legs. Remember that in a combi, if someone in the back wants to get out, everyone in the front has to get out too.

It was incredibly hot inside the combi, and sitting squeezed between two other passengers, I was not exactly comfortable. My knees hurt from sitting in one position for so long. My back is strong, so that did not bother me. I had brought water and oranges and some dark chocolate to eat, dark chocolate being my antidote for whatever ails me, but the chocolate melted. Fortunately, I was able to buy food and water during the trip.

We reached Windhoek at 9:30 pm. The combi did not go to a central point, such as The Station in Gaborone. It stopped at a gas station in central Windhoek, but a gas station which had closed for the night. I thought that there might be cabs there to meet us, but I did not see any. I tried to ask some of the Pentecostals for help, but they all melted away, picked up by friends and family. Finally no one was left except a man with a small red car which looked as if it had seen better days. I had my phone with me, but I did not know the Namibia equivalent of 911 nor any other Namibian phone number. The guy with the car claimed to be a cab driver, and although I was seriously afraid, I did not have much choice. I asked him to drive me to the hotel, telling him I knew where it was. I could see it at the intersection of two highways in the distance, even in the dark.

I asked the man how much he would charge, to show that I was not a total innocent, and off we went, fortunately without incident. I arrived at the hotel, quite a nice one with a fancy name: Fürstenhof. But I think that they had given away my room. The room they gave me looked as if some drunks had had a fight in there. One of the bedside tables had collapsed, the frame of the bed was damaged on that side, so that the bed sloped, and there was a large spot on the carpet that looked as if someone had tried to bleach it. There was no other room available, and the restaurant had closed for the night. I snacked on my leftover food, except the chocolate which had totally melted into the paper in which I tried to wrap it, and looked forward to the excellent Protea breakfast in the morning.

In the morning I walked to the city centre where I strolled through the touristy town centre with craft dealers' tables on the streets and an arcade which included a German-language drugstore. I returned to the hotel in good time to catch a taxi to the airport for the flight to Gaborone, one of the first direct flights between the two cities, except that I almost didn't make it. The taxi was late; the driver explained that he needed to pick his children up from school. Didn't Windhoek have taxi drivers without children? And then he needed gas, and the first three stations we tried had run out of gas. Now that never happened in Botswana.

The Windhoek airport is far from the city, 40 km, and we arrived there just in time for the flight. The explanation for the location of the airport is that when the South Africans ruled Namibia (from 1919 to 1990), for security reasons they wanted an airport as far east as possible from the city. If SWAPO (the national liberation movement) took Windhoek, the South Africans wanted to be able to get away before SWAPO reached the airport. Surely that would have depended on the direction from which the SWAPO forces were coming and the speed at which they were travelling, but who was I to question the logic of the apartheid government.

Gentle reader, I did not attempt to tell you about all of my travels in southern Africa, to Zambia to see Victoria Falls, to Swakopmund in Namibia and Durban in South Africa. I just included a few highlights. And of those, the combi ride from Lüderitz to Windhoek surely was the highest and the lightest. I had travelled like a local person, with the local people, for 700 km and survived to tell this tale. Not everything went well. Air Namibia did not refund me for the return trip via South Africa that I had taken care to cancel. That was unfortunate. You can't win them all. I had the memory of the combi ride: I had travelled like a real African.

CHAPTER 4   MAN, WOMAN, SEX

My friend Tom once quoted an expatriate jurist from the independence era who famously said, "A Motswana woman is like a bridge; anyone can cross." (That magistrate was quickly sent back to Ghana.) That statement may be true, at least in part, but it is also misleading.

Botswana is a profoundly Christian country. Immigrants might be Muslims, Sikhs or Hindus, but nearly every local person declares herself or himself to be a Christian, and the many churches are full on Sundays (See Chapter 5.)

But this Christianity includes hardly any of the once-dominant Christian view that sex is an original sin. Nineteenth-century missionaries struggled with what to them seemed an anomaly. It was not difficult to convince the locals to adopt a belief in the Christian god and the wickedness of liquor, but try as they would, they could not convince them of the virtues of monogamy and the evils of premarital and extramarital sex.

In that sense one could describe Botswana as a Freudian paradise. Sex (and for that matter death) are a part of life. So are children. It took me some time to discover that a large number of the female undergraduates had children, usually only one. In class all these young women appeared to be regular young people, in their late teens or early twenties, who were perhaps a little immature for their age. But once the university term had finished, and one of these students came in to pick up a paper or ask for a reference, she was often accompanied by a little child. Occasionally that child would be a younger sibling, but usually it was her own, which during the term had been entrusted to the care of a female relative, a mother or an auntie. The student/mother and — if he could be found and was willing — the father, was expected to make a monthly contribution to the expenses incurred by the caregiver.

Now you might think that children raised away from their parents and sometimes transferred from relative to relative might grow up with psychological problems, but this appears not to be the case. This is how many children are raised in Botswana, and if the caregivers accept it as normal, I guess the children do too.

Of course there were exceptions: female undergraduates who did not have children and boys who accepted that they had some responsibility for the children they had fathered. I knew a student who had an interesting task to perform once a month. Her brother in South Africa would send her a special baby formula that his former girlfriend's baby needed. The student would go to a designated combi stop to pick up the formula and then deliver it to the mother for her baby.

One of our teaching assistants was a tall, dark, handsome Kalanga guy. One day, when a colleague and I visited a new mall in search of a fancy coffee shop, we encountered Lawrence leading a little two-year-old boy by the hand. He said that this was his and his girlfriend's child, and sometimes on Saturday he would look after the little boy, to give the mother a break. My colleague was so impressed! She said that it would not have occurred to most Batswana men that a mother might need a break.

On the other hand, many men (though by no means all) enjoyed spending time with their children. In the malls on the weekends there were men shopping with their little kids, or bouncing them on their knees on one of the benches while the mothers did the shopping. Syntax loved to play with Jason. When the taxi business was slow, he would go home to be with his children. Sarah commented on what a good father Syntax was.

If she had the means, a single mother might stay single and raise her children on her own. Or she might marry the father of the most recent child or someone else, but in either case all her children become part of the new family. Though there were exceptions, stepmothers and stepfathers did not seem to have the bad reputation that they have among people of European descent. My driver Syntax came from a family where his mother had died when he was a toddler. His father married another woman who had children from a previous marriage, and then his father and the new wife had more children. They all thought of each other as brothers and sisters, and there seemed to be little distinction among them.

Still, not everyone was so casual about single motherhood. In Chapter 1, I told you about the undergraduate who befriended me after she saw me hobbling around on my broken toe. The following April, at exam time, she stayed with me for two weeks.

Bayapo belonged to a fundamentalist church based in South Africa, the ZCC or Zionist Christian Church. Unlike the members of other fundamentalist churches, where the women might go to church in a blouse with a plunging neckline, ZCC women were expected to cover their hair with a kind of turban and to wear long skirts, although these rules were not strictly enforced for someone working in an environment, say a retail store or a restaurant, where such an outfit might be out of place.

During my last couple of months in Botswana, I asked Bayapo to come over, so that we could cook a meal together, just like old times. While we were in the kitchen, her phone buzzed with a text message. She shouted with delight, "My wonderful daughter. She came first in her class." I was totally flabbergasted. You have a daughter, I said, a daughter who is old enough to go to school. Yes, she said, she just completed the first grade. She is staying with my auntie in our home town of Francistown.

The moral of this story is not that Bayapo had a daughter, but that she had kept that fact from me when there surely would have been many an occasion to tell me about it.

Although monogamy is the law in Botswana when it comes to formal marriage, the idea that it is an unnatural practice is deeply engrained in the culture. This applies to women as well as men, though there is a little more tolerance toward married men who sleep around. The following quotation from Unity Dow's novel *The Screaming of the Innocent* describes a typical situation and the accompanying attitudes.

Cleavage at a gospel concert

Syntax's and Sarah's wedding in July 2014; in front are
their three children, Lesly, Leticia and Jason

Motlatsi was a woman in her thirties, a teacher who was active in her community. She had had five children with a partner who

> ... was showing no inclination towards marrying her. He'd seemed to be comfortable with the arrangement, whereby he slept and ate at his parents' house but had no demands placed on him to help within that home. Occasionally, he'd spent nights at his other girlfriend's house. At first, that aspect hadn't been a major problem because he'd been discreet — and anyway, everyone knows a man can't be with just one woman.... The problem had assumed serious proportions when he'd become less discreet.

Discretion seems to be the nub of the matter. Sleeping around in moderation is accepted, but it needs to be discreet. One of my colleagues was recently divorced. Others told me that his wife had been quite promiscuous while he was out of the country studying for his PhD. That seemed to be all right, but she persevered in that behaviour after he came back. He then decided that there was no solution but a divorce.

That said, not all husbands or boyfriends are willing to forgive or forget. In the papers there were plenty of stories of domestic abuse or murders of wives or girlfriends, some of them alcohol-induced, but some presumably caused by jealousy. During the Easter season in 2012, I went to see a new and much-praised outdoor play called "The Passion Play". It consisted of three short plays, each one introduced by a young boy who shouted into the hills, "Jesus! Jesus!" suggesting that Jesus was not to be found. The third play consisted of the story of a rich middle-aged man who had married a pretty young wife. An evil spirit in human form told the husband that the wife had been seen performing at a strip club, which was not true. When the wife came home from a shopping trip, the husband choked and killed her. I assume that the moral of the story was: Where is Jesus when such events can happen? But the story also told me that jealous husbands exist, even amid the relaxed sexual mores of Botswana.

In parts of Africa, such as Somalia, Senegal and Egypt, the fear of female sexuality is so great that women are mutilated by an operation that is misleadingly called female circumcision, an operation designed to make sexual pleasure impossible and intercourse painful. This, of course, is very different from what happens in southern Africa. I wouldn't say that most women revel in their sexuality, but female sexuality is a normal part of life. Deeply plunging necklines are common, especially in the warm summer months. At the cultural village south of Gaborone, the guides tell you that in a traditional village, a man would choose his bride by watching the women from behind as they danced around a fire wearing loincloths. The most appealing rear end would win someone's heart.

It is also accepted that women as well as men can initiate contacts that lead to sex. I read a newspaper story about a taxi rank located near a secondary school. The taxi drivers complained of being pestered by advances from the female students. When I returned to Botswana for a visit in 2014, I asked to see one of the military officers whom I had taught in 2012. Another officer told me that GG had been discharged and was now unemployed. The official reason given was a conviction for driving under the influence, but my informant thought that such a conviction without an accident was not a sufficient reason. GG had been an instructor for female recruits and had been warned against any sexual relations with them, but my informant continued, some of those women can be pretty persistent. (GG sued for wrongful dismissal – and won. He was reinstated with his former rank and salary. I don't think that there are many countries where you can sue the armed forces for wrongful dismissal.)

At the University, the younger and good-looking male professors complained of advances from female students, such as why don't you come to my room in the hostel to help me study. When I was team teaching a course with a young and good-looking lecturer, one of the girls came up to me after class and asked me to ask my colleague if he was available. I assured her that he had a fiancée, but she persisted, and I did pass on the message, albeit jokingly.

This is not to say that the more common problem of male professors pursuing female students does not exist. It undoubtedly does, as it does elsewhere, but I must say that I only noticed a few instances. One of my colleagues, an older gentleman, not a Motswana but some-one who had lived in the country for thirty years, enough time to be well acculturated, fell seriously ill, and it soon became obvious that he would not be able to return to teaching. Being the good person I am, I offered to sort out his office. Amid the twenty-year-old minutes of long forgotten committee meetings, I found seven condoms. These condoms were not just freebies from hotel rooms that a frugal man might have picked up for future use, though they might have been that too. Each one was in its original packaging, then wrapped in a neatly folded piece of scrap paper, and the resultant little package was then placed in an airmail envelope which had been carefully licked and sealed. I assumed he used airmail envelopes because they have a bright blue and red edge and can be readily identified in case of need. The envelopes were scattered about in various file drawers. Perhaps the old man knew where they were, or perhaps he scattered them about like squirrels bury nuts, so that one would be handy in case of need.

I saw few public displays of affection, even among the students on campus, just the occasional cuddle on a bench near the library. Once, in the Main Mall, in a fast-food restaurant, I saw a young man reach across the table to plunge his hand into the plunging neckline of the girl sitting across from him. She brushed him off with a horrified expression.

In the mid-1990s, HIV/AIDS fell into this Freudian paradise of easy sexual relations like a meteor from the sky. Soon people, young people in their twenties, thirties and forties, were dying by the hundreds. There were funerals every Saturday; by 2004 there were so many funerals that some had to be held on other days; the orphanages filled with children whose parents were no longer able to care for them; many grandmothers were left to care for the numerous offspring of their infected children. Worse yet, many babies were born with the disease, which sentenced them to an early death at the age of five or six. Soon Botswana and Swaziland were vying for an unenviable title: the highest incidence of HIV/AIDS of any country in the world.

Worst of all was the fact that among a people who regarded sex and pregnancy as a normal part of life, HIV/AIDS became a shame that no one wanted to discuss or admit to having, a circumstance that meant that transmission became all the easier. In my three years in the country, I did not meet a single person who admitted to being HIV-positive, and that in spite of the fact that one-third of young adults are infected. Still I was able to make a few guesses.

There was a rumour that one of our colleagues was infected. All I noticed was that he was very careful about what he ate, but that could have been a sign of diabetes, another scourge of contemporary Botswana. One of my female graduate students came down with a flu that soon became a pneumonia that almost killed her. I assumed that was also due to a lack of antibodies, i.e. HIV. When I came back from Canada in 2012 and tried to make an appointment with my hairdresser, I was told that she had died of meningitis. A few weeks later, a colleague's brother died of meningitis. When I expressed surprise that so many middle-aged people were contracting what in Canada was usually a children's disease, a graduate student told me that it was HIV/AIDS that was causing middle-aged people to succumb to this disease. Another colleague told me that her sister had had to deliver her first child by Caesarean section and that she would be unable to breastfeed. This was a dead giveaway: HIV-positive women need Caesareans because HIV can be transmitted in the birth canal, and breast milk also passes on the virus.

Everyone, including me, likes to complain of the inefficiency of Botswana's bureaucracy. If I had to stereotype a people I have come to admire, I must say that a penchant toward bureaucracy is a Tswana characteristic. That said, I must also admit that the government of Botswana has done amazingly well in coping with a health crisis that has defied other African governments. It succeeded in tapping a number of resources, including the Merck and Gates Foundations, Harvard University, the Baylor School of Medicine, and the American government itself, which contributed funds and expertise by means of the PEPFAR program and sent Peace Corps volunteers to help with community outreach.

As a result every Botswana citizen who self-identifies as HIV-positive now has access to ARV treatment at no cost, and testing is free and widely available. However, treatment is not available to non-citizens, and this is a special problem for the many legal and illegal immigrants from Zimbabwe. (The government has, however, decided to give ARVs to foreigners in prison.) There are special programs for HIV-positive pregnant women, and there is an American-sponsored clinic where HIV-positive children are taught to take their meds. There are radio and television spots urging people to get tested, advocating the use of condoms and urging pregnant women to go to the doctor early in their pregnancy, so that transmission can be prevented. Sometimes after the evening news, BTV ran a kind of soap opera drama that included a good girl who went for couples testing with her fiancé before they went to get their marriage license and a bad girl who was lured to a hotel room by an older man who promised her a fancy cell phone if she would have sex without a condom. Billboards showed a traditional Tswana couple with the message, "There is a Botswana saying that you must not ask a man where he has been. But because of HIV you must." Another billboard showed about twenty male and female faces connected by lines running all over the place. The message was "Who's in your sexual network?" I did not find this second billboard effective. It was designed by an American advertising agency, and in the US a sexual network is a bad thing, smacking of promiscuity. This is not the case in Botswana. The billboards had English labelling in the centre of the city, and Setswana labelling in the suburbs.

Condoms are supposed to be available in public washrooms, but the dispensers in the university washrooms are usually empty. Hotel rooms, on the other hand, do have condoms discreetly placed in a drawer, sometimes near the Gideon Bible. At one time the local supermarket had a colourful display of condoms on the customer service counter, where they also sold cigarettes, telephone cards and the more expensive items such as face creams. The display was removed in a couple of weeks, perhaps because it offended some sensibilities.

On campus, there was a student association called the Society for the Prevention of HIV/AIDS, and signs inviting students to their meetings could be found along walls and on bulletin boards together with signs for other student associations, such as basketball clubs and the law society. Society meetings usually featured speakers who could educate members on a relevant issue. The announcement for one meeting sticks in my mind. The topic was "Can you catch HIV/AIDS from oral sex? (blow-job)". I was curious but never had the nerve to attend one of the meetings to see who or how many people went there.

Another problem was that at first men especially resisted getting tested for HIV. I was told that when the University held a testing clinic almost all the participants were women. Hence all the publicity calling for "couples testing". On one occasion the University held a testing clinic and offered free tickets to a concert by a popular South African pop star to any couples who attended the clinic.

In spite of all these efforts, the infection rate remains stubbornly high. Botswana still has the second-highest incidence of HIV infections in the world (after Swaziland). There has been some improvement. Fewer children are born HIV-positive, to the point where the Baylor clinic for children has now turned to the counselling of adolescents. The government claims that the number of new infections is decreasing. If this is true, it should show up in future statistics. The government is also hoping that the wide distribution of ARVs will reduce the rate of transmission since men or women who are taking the medication are less likely to pass on the disease. Recent studies have also shown that circumcised men are less likely to contract the disease from infected women. As circumcision was also a component of traditional male initiation rites, now largely fallen into disuse, there are few cultural inhibitions against the procedure. The problem is that both the meds and circumcision make transmission less likely, but do not eliminate the possibility of it happening. They can thus create a false sense of security.

So government and people soldier on, HIV and all. The life expectancy is now 53 years, still far below that of Russia and

Bangladesh, who for all their problems, have a life expectancy of 69 years. And so far there is no evidence which would show that the incidence of the dreadful disease is decreasing.

As the billboard I mentioned above demonstrates, the traditional Motswana male was the king in his castle. He could come and go as he liked, and the women of the household were expected to obey. But things are changing. Many women are now educated and expect to be treated with some respect. There was much agonizing about the fact that only four women were members of parliament; women are also seriously underrepresented in municipal government and all but absent from tribal councils. At the University, I met a lecturer who was the next in line for the tribal chieftainship of a small tribe based in the village of Kang. The council did not want to appoint her because of her gender, and last I heard the matter was still unresolved.

Outside of the elected branch of government, however, women have done well. At the University there are many female professors, some deans and one vice-president. There are many women in managerial positions in the banks. There seem to be a fair number of female doctors, and women are not only teachers, they are also principals of schools. My graduate classes consisted largely of senior bureaucrats studying part-time, and at least half of them were women. One of them has now become an assistant deputy minister.

Of course, there will always be extremes of men- or women-dominated families. This is the case in Botswana as it is anywhere else. I had one colleague who was a professor who also had administrative duties, whose husband expected her to be home for lunch every day. Given the quality of the food available at UB, a number of colleagues did go home for lunch, but this lady hardly ever stayed except when there was a meeting right after lunch. She had four children, and when these children were still quite young — in the 5-12 year range — she won a scholarship to study toward her PhD in Europe. The husband did not want the responsibility for the children, even though three of them were boys. So she took them with her, all four, and with great self-discipline worked on her thesis during the week. On the weekends she took the children on excursions to learn about local history and culture.

Another colleague, a man, has a wife who is an engineer and is studying part-time for her MBA. They have three children, ranging in age from two to nineteen. This man is proud of his accomplished wife, and though he has senior administrative responsibilities at UB, he goes home to baby-sit when his wife has a late meeting or will, if possible, work from home when the maid is away.

These are cases that are not so different from what happens in Canada. On average there is not so much difference in the roles of the sexes among educated people.

One factor which no doubt helps to boost the status of women is the system of *bogadi* (also called *lebola*) or "bride price") In South Asia, women are considered a burden, and their fathers have to pay a prospective husband a considerable amount of money (a dowry) to compensate the groom's family for taking on such a burden. In Africa south of the Sahara, the opposite is the case. A man must pay a bride price, usually calculated as a sum of money equivalent to an agreed number of cattle, to his prospective bride's family. This system is prevalent among sub-Saharan Africans, even among educated people. When one of my colleague's sons got married, the colleague boasted of how high a bride price he had paid. And when the President of South Africa married for a fifth time, his bride price was officially registered with the appropriate court. (South Africans may marry up to four wives whereas Batswana are restricted to one. President Zuma was able to marry a fifth wife because he had divorced the first.)

In Botswana, the bride price is officially registered with the tribal authorities under tribal law. It is possible to go to the local courthouse and marry without the exchange of a bride price, but it is unheard of if both man and wife are from the same tribe. And even if they are not, the man is expected to pay the bride price. Indeed the price is even higher if the bride is not from the same tribe. All that said, some educated people do break with tradition to marry without the payment of a bride price.

Bride prices, like dowries, have grown faster than inflation, which means that many poorer men cannot afford to marry. That is where the relaxed sexual mores of Botswana come in handy. Couples can live together and raise children without being married and hardly anyone will raise an eyebrow. The problem arises if the father dies without providing for the children by means of a will or a life insurance policy. In that case, the wife and children of a couple who are not formally married lose all their inheritance rights, and the dead man's property goes to his blood relatives. Botswana has no inheritance provisions for common-law couples.

Abortion is illegal in Botswana unless the life of the mother is in imminent danger. Homosexuality is illegal too, but neither law is enforced. Hospitals do not perform abortions, but I have been told that there are ads in the papers for "womb cleaning" in private clinics. If that is allowed to continue, the law on abortion will be as dead a letter as the one on homosexuality. (It seems especially cruel to forbid abortion when there is a good chance that a child will be born with HIV.)

Homosexual acts are illegal in most African countries (but notably not in South Africa). However, while that law is enforced, sometimes brutally, in most of those countries, including even Namibia which used to be governed by South Africa, that is not the case in Botswana. There is an association which lobbies for the rights of gays and lesbians, and it advertises its meetings in the newspapers. When I first came to Botswana, a graduate student who asked me to supervise his MA thesis felt obliged to tell me that he had lived with the same housemate for thirteen years. Of course, it made no difference to me whom he lived with.

The President of Botswana, Ian Khama, is widely rumoured to be homosexual. He is not married, and the rumour has never been publicly denied. Once there was a story in the leading national paper about a South Indian supermarket manager who turned down the offer of a Motswana bride, saying, "I am like your president. I only f**k men." When I read that, I thought that the speaker would soon be deported.

Only a few months earlier, another supermarket manager who was married to a Motswana and who had made some offhand comment about the president, not of a sexual nature, was deported for insulting the head of state.

> *Background fact: Many Indian businessmen in Botswana marry local women and put the business in the wife's name. In this way, the business will have access to any privileges reserved for citizens of Botswana.*

But this time, the man who turned down the offer of a Motswana bride was charged and the case sent to trial. A few weeks later, when the case came up in court, a newspaper headline read "President's Sexuality Questioned in Court." After that, the trial was moved behind closed doors, and I was not able to find out what happened to the supermarket manager.

> *Anecdote: During the 2014 election campaign in Botswana, the President was photographed with an attractive tall woman. One of my friends, a supporter of the governing party, said cynically, "He gets himself photographed with a lady. After the election, everything will be back to normal."*

The outdoor play I saw in April 2012 included an episode which gave an indication of the evolving attitudes toward homosexuality. The episode began once again with a little boy calling "Jesus! Jesus!" to the rocky hills behind the stage. The story was about a widower and his two teen-aged children. The older, a boy, had won a debating contest and been given the prize by the mayor who commented favourably on the young man's prospects. The sister and the father were so proud of their debater and dreamed of his bright political future. The play was well written and well-acted; you could tell that the three of them were very close.

Then the father learns that the boy is gay. He angrily chases him from the house, calling his behaviour disgusting. A year later, the boy phones home, telling his father how much he misses him and that he would like to come back to the family home. The father rebuffs him but soon changes his mind. He tries to find his son to tell him that he is welcome to come back. But it is too late; the young man has killed himself.

> *Update: In November 2014 a court in Botswana ruled that the NGO representing gay and lesbian persons had the right to register as an NGO, as other organizations do, such as those defending human rights, women's rights and environmental issues. This in effect strikes down the law outlawing male homosexual acts.*

A note about President Khama: he is as authoritarian as he can get away with under Botswana's constitution, and he has a strong Puritan streak, perhaps learned from his English mother. He, for example, keeps trying to increase the taxes on alcoholic drinks. Once the local brewery took him to court, and the court found that Khama had not followed the constitution when he tried to raise the alcohol tax. But instead of taking the tax increase to parliament, as he should have done, Khama worked out a deal with the brewery whereby the government imposed a lesser tax increase.

Another example of the President's puritanical behaviour caused some amusement. Batswana ladies are fond of deeply plunging necklines, to the point where it would sometimes appear that a nipple might pop out at any minute. This may be a remnant of pre-colonial times when unmarried women would go topless. The President issued a decree that all women working for the government must wear tops that did not show cleavage. And for good measure, and probably so as not to appear too sexist, the decree added that men should not go to work wearing the little floppy hats of which Batswana men are so fond. After a few weeks the ladies' necklines started creeping down again. I'm not sure about the hats.

One couple whose relationship I was able to observe was that of my driver Syntax and his partner Sarah. They were an interesting couple because they had both grown up in a village and now lived in the city, which is the case for most Batswana. Before she had children, Sarah had worked as a store clerk at Woolworths. Syntax worked at the University as a clerk and data-entry person, and since that job did not make enough money to support a family, he also worked as a cab driver on Saturdays and on most weekday evenings. Syntax's most recent car, a six-seater Mazda, was his most valuable and prized possession. Both Syntax and Sarah had completed junior school but had not continued on to senior secondary school, which meant that they had about a Grade 10 education and spoke reasonably good English. On longer trips, Syntax would try to teach me some Setswana, and I would try to help him with his English.

> *Background note: Gentle reader, you may be wondering how someone could be given a name such as Syntax. His real first name is Etsogile. His football coach in junior school — an Englishman — could not say that name (pronounced Aetsorileh), so he made up the name Syntax, and it stuck.*

When I needed a driver each evening to take me from the café back to the bed-and-breakfast, I soon learned that every driver wanted me to take his phone number and make him my regular driver. I settled on four regular drivers: Syntax, Modise, Robert and Kitso, but Syntax became my driver of choice. He spoke reasonably good English, was usually available when I needed him, and because he also worked at UB, he knew the University well. He and I bonded when I broke my toe and called him from the Private Hospital at eleven in the evening. He had already gone to sleep, but he got up to come and fetch me. I had been visiting an Indian family and was wearing a Punjabi suit. When I came out of the hospital hobbling on my bandaged foot, Syntax did not ask, "What you have done to your foot?" He said, "You are wearing such a beautiful dress, Prof."

In those days, Syntax lived in Gaborone all by himself. He and Sarah had left their oldest boy in the village with Sarah's mother, so that Sarah could work. It is common for city people who work to leave their children with relatives in the village. This gives the relatives a cash income, and allows the parents to work in the city. When we visited Syntax's village, we met an auntie who kept six or seven children who appeared to be from two to ten years old. She was a happy and smiling auntie because the board paid by so many city relatives gave her a good income by village standards. And I must say, the children did look well dressed, well fed and happy.

But then Sarah got pregnant with their second child. She returned to the village to have the child, though the baby was actually born in a nearby hospital (no home births for Syntax and Sarah). This is where the story becomes mysterious. After their second child Jason was born, on October 2, 2008, Sarah stayed in the village. She was still there in February 2009. One day Syntax told me that he had some good news: Sarah's parents had "released" her, and she and the baby would be returning to Gaborone to live with him. That month he also borrowed 2000P from me, which he paid back on the next payday.

Now I think that there may have been some connection between the money and the "release". But Syntax would not say anything about that. He is modern enough to know that some of the traditional practices might appear weird or wrong to me, but not modern enough to defy those conventions.

> *Background note: There is a Tswana superstition that a father should not see his newborn for the first couple of months. That is one reason women return to their home town or village to have their babies. The Alexander McCall Smith novel* The Minor Adjustment Beauty Salon *includes an episode about a couple who successfully defied that convention. Syntax certainly did not follow it in the case of his third child; I don't know about the second.*

So Sarah returned to Gaborone. After Sarah and infant Jason had settled in, I did the Canadian thing and invited all three of them over for dinner. I asked Bayapo too because I knew that she would be a great help in the kitchen. Sarah is seriously overweight — a woman of traditional stature — but Jason is the cutest little boy. I am not one to dote on babies, but I have fallen in love with Jason, who is bright, smart and sociable. Syntax adores him. As Sarah herself points out, Syntax is an excellent father. Maybe it is because his mother died when he was so little, or perhaps that is just the way he is. He loves to play with Jason, calling him *monna*, Setswana for man.

The few times that I have seen Syntax with Lesly, the older boy, it seems to me that their relationship is more reserved. Lesly, like Syntax, loves to play soccer, but he also excels in school. In Botswana, children are ranked according to their academic achievements, and Lesly stands first in his class most of the time. If I may be allowed a bit of pop psychology, he may be overachieving not only because he is the oldest child, but also because he may feel abandoned, being left behind in the village. I don't quite understand why he stayed there when his mother and little brother are in Gaborone. It may be because the money Syntax pays for his keep is cash income for Sarah's mother, or it may be that he is some kind of a hostage, kept in the village until Syntax comes up with the bride price and marries Sarah (which he finally did do in July 2014. In October 2015, after Lesly has completed primary school, he will come to live in Gaborone with his nuclear family.)

> *Extra information: I contacted what is reputed to be the best private school in Gaborone to see if there was any chance of getting a scholarship for Lesly. The principal, a New Englander, was sympathetic, but said that Lesly was not disadvantaged enough to be eligible for a scholarship. He has two parents and a father with a reasonably good income. On the other hand, the fees for that school are higher than Syntax's monthly salary. The principal has promised that Lesly could have access to some of the school's facilities, notably the library. That will be good for Lesly because Syntax's family lives within walking distance of that upscale school. Lesly will start his academic career in Gaborone by going to one of the government-run junior schools.*

On my birthday in November 2009, I invited Syntax and Sarah to come to the coffee shop in Riverwalk for an iced coffee, which neither one of them had ever tasted. On that same day, Thibaud, an intern from the French embassy who was nearing the end of his term, had organized an exhibition of posters produced by South African anti-apartheid artists who had fled to Botswana during that sad time in history. The exhibit was at the National Museum and was to be followed by a talk and a dinner. I asked Syntax to pick me up from the museum after the dinner. Everything happened on African, not French, time. By the time Syntax, Sarah and Jason came to pick me up, the talk was just over and the tour of the exhibit had not yet begun. So I asked them to come in and join us. Syntax hesitated, saying, "Let me check this out," but Sarah had no hesitation and marched right in. I was glad that Jason was wearing a diaper.

By that time, quite a few of the original attendees had left. We walked through the exhibit, and Syntax and Sarah were happy to find there was a poster painted by an artist from their tribe. Since the attendance had dwindled, I was sure that there would be more than enough food for dinner. I asked Syntax and Sarah to stay, and we had dinner, sitting on a little stone fence near the serving area. They enjoyed their diplomatic meal of rice and creamed chicken, and then we went out for iced coffee.

As I observed their relationship, I came to the conclusion that Sarah and Syntax have a lot of respect for one another. I don't think that Syntax fits into the Tswana stereotype of the philandering husband. For one thing, what with his two jobs, his football coaching commitment, and his family responsibilities, he would hardly have time (or money) for anyone else. But he also has a lot of respect for Sarah. When she did not want to do something, as for example drive the car, he would simply tell me, "She refused!" Syntax is not a man of many words.

Sarah respects the fact that Syntax is a good father, and she is happy to be living in Gaborone and away from the village with all of its social restrictions (not to mention the lack of electricity). There is a lot of rampant romanticism about village life out there, not only in Botswana but all over the world, from Grey's "Elegy in a Country Churchyard" to André Gide's stories to the novel *Heidi* and to Mahatma Gandhi, but if the truth be told, most people prefer to live in cities. According to the UN, more than half of the world's people now live in cities.

Syntax wanted to start a taxi company, with Sarah as his first driver in addition to himself. To that end, he bought a second car, but Sarah was not enthusiastic about the project. While they had the two cars, I tried my best to persuade Sarah to drive me from time to time. As Syntax pointed out, she would be primarily responsible for driving his regular lady customers. But that is not what Sarah wanted to do. There are hardly any women cab drivers in Botswana, and Sarah was not interested in being a feminist pioneer. Eventually the older of the two cars died a natural death, and with it the project of making Sarah a driving partner. She did still occasionally drive me when Syntax was at work or playing soccer.

During Sarah's brief driving career, the day came when we were driving down the road in both cars, Syntax at the wheel of one and Sarah in the other. I was in Sarah's car. My phone rang. It was Syntax, making an illegal call while driving. Besides, it was unheard-of for Syntax to use his precious airtime to talk to me. He usually allowed my phone to ring just once or twice, expecting me to call back after I had seen his number. But this time he barked into the phone, "Tell her to drive in the outside lane. The inside lane is for passing." She stayed in the centre lane.

In September 2010, Syntax and Sarah decided to send Jason back to the village to live with Lesly and Sarah's mother. Sarah would be free to go back to work as a sales clerk. I felt sorry for Jason and objected strenuously, pointing out that after they paid Sarah's mother for the room and board, there would not be much left of Sarah's wages. But they said that their mind was made up and, of course, it was their decision. So one weekend they took Jason to the village. I am sure that Syntax missed him. They phoned home a couple of times a week to see how he was doing, and Syntax told me pathetic stories, such as that Jason ran to the window every time a car came by and called out "Papa! Papa!"

After six weeks, Syntax and Sarah went to the village and brought Jason back. They told me that it was because of me, but I don't believe that for a minute. There must have been another reason or combination of reasons. Maybe Sarah's mother no longer felt up to looking after a small child or perhaps Sarah did not really want to go to work or maybe Syntax also missed Jason. Anyway, Jason was happy to be back, and I was happy to see him back. I organized a belated second birthday party for him; I have a lovely picture of Syntax holding Jason as he tries to cut the birthday cake.

I was concerned about what would happen to Sarah and the children if Syntax was hurt or injured in a car accident. As long as they were not married, the children had no inheritance rights. True, Syntax did not own much, primarily his car and furniture. But even that would have gone to his brothers. So I started a campaign to persuade them to get married. They did want to get married. But here we ran into another problem. Marrying meant paying the bride price, which in their case meant the equivalent of seven cows or 14 000P plus the cost of the wedding and presents for all the aunts and uncles, a dress for each aunt and a blanket for each uncle, which altogether would add up to over 20 000P or $2500, money that Syntax did not have.

Still Syntax tried to begin negotiations toward a marriage. He came back from the village with a long list of uncles and aunts that would need to be given presents. But apart from the fact that Syntax did not have the money, there still was no wedding date because there was a problem with Sarah's father who was supposed to be a key person in setting the wedding date. The father had deserted the family and moved to South Africa where he was working in the mines. He showed up about once a year to inspect his family, and it was on one of those visits that the extended family came up with the list of required "presents". But he did not show up again to help set a wedding date.

Then in 2011, while I was in Canada, one more reason emerged why Sarah might not have wanted to go to work. She wanted a third child, a girl if at all possible. Syntax said, OK, but this is it: no more children. And luckily for them Sarah did produce a baby girl, Leticia, in July. As babies go, she is a nice little girl, pleasant, and does not cry too much, but she is not as cute as Jason.

Now Syntax's inheritance problems had become much worse, and at the same time, there was an increase in the bride price. A third child made Sarah more valuable. And there was no sign of the putative but absent father-in-law. When I left in December 2012, Syntax was talking about a wedding soon. I made a grand gesture by having the wedding dress made for Sarah. One reason I did that was that I noticed that tradespeople such as seamstresses charged village people such as Sarah more than they did me. I once had to prevent Sarah getting royally ripped off by a Ghanaian seamstress. This is odd because in India it is the foreigners who are overcharged. (Sarah and I would go to the seamstress together because it is nice to have another woman with you when you are trying on clothes).

Anyway when Syntax told me that the wedding dress would cost 5000P, I took charge. I went to the seamstress's hole-in-the-wall shop and negotiated the price down to 3800P. The dress was made, but I did not have time to see it before I left. I just hoped that Sarah would not gain too much weight before the magic wedding day arrived. (She didn't; see the wedding photo in this chapter.)

In the absence of a valid village wedding, registered according to tribal law, Sarah and their children had no inheritance rights to whatever property Syntax owned. (In Botswana there is a kind of pseudo-federalism that gives the tribal authorities the right to deal with family law, property rights, land use and petty crime, subject to the overall provisions of the national human rights code.) When Syntax's own father had died, most of the family property — primarily land, because the family was not wealthy enough to own cattle or even goats — had been given to the oldest and youngest sons. Syntax, one of the middle children, got very little.

True, Syntax had a generous life insurance policy by virtue of his status as an employee of UB. He had named the beneficiaries. He was allowed to assign the pay out of that policy in percentages, and he assured me that he had left a sizeable amount to Sarah with the rest going to his elder sister, who had helped to raise him and who now lived on the family farm where she did subsistence farming with no cash income of her own.

Since the formal village wedding was as far away as ever — one could say three steps forward and four steps back — I suggested that Syntax and Sarah go to the local court house in Gaborone and have a quiet court wedding. No one in their village need know about it, and they could have their village wedding later. My urbanite Batswana friends assured me that such a thing was possible, but Syntax insisted that he could not do such a thing. If people in the village ever found out — and they were bound to find out once the village wedding took place — he and Sarah would be ostracized for the rest of their lives.

Well, I said, if you cannot get married now, why don't you make a will leaving your property to Sarah and the children? Syntax liked that idea, but this would mean drawing up a valid will. The law school at UB had assigned one professor with a full-time secretary to help members of staff with minor legal issues. He helped me a couple of times when I needed documents notarized. But what was good for full professors from abroad obviously was not good for clerks in the finance department. The secretary told me that wills were such a simple matter that an undergraduate student would send me a model will with blanks to fill in — but it took said undergraduate student several weeks to send me the form. By that time it was close to my departure date, so that Syntax and I never managed to find the time to sit down and work on it. And that's where things rested until the wedding in July 2014.

Sarah tries hard to be a good wife and mother. She informs herself of medical and nutritional advice. She is careful to give the children healthy food. The children were up-to-date with all their vaccinations, though the government does not give Batswana any choice. The basic childhood vaccinations are compulsory.

Sarah belongs to one of the many fundamentalist churches and sometimes reads the Bible while she is watching TV. She enjoys going to church, but does not get to go often because Syntax is seldom available for babysitting on Sundays, and Jason has little tolerance for a three- or four-hour church service, which is what some of the local fundamentalist churches expect of their congregation. Syntax does not go to church. He says that he can be a good person without going to church.

Syntax works at two jobs. During normal office hours, he is supposed to be a clerk in the finance department of the University, but that job also involves driving to the bank to make deposits. Gradually the driving component increased while the clerking component decreased. Syntax asked to be paid as a driver, which would mean more money. After some discussion, and several months later, the University decided that they would advertise the position of driver and then Syntax could apply for it. In the meantime he was doing the driving and being paid as a clerk. Then he got a better-paid job in the printing department, meaning that the finance department will have to find themselves another driver.

Anyway, that is Syntax's day job. On most evenings and on Saturdays, he is a cab driver. With seven or eight others he hangs around the restaurant exit at Riverwalk looking for business, except that he has quite a few regular customers, like me, who call him when they need a ride. There is not much money to be made from us local customers, who just want to go home after a meal or a bit of shopping. The real money comes from people who want to go to one of the outer suburbs or a nearby village. Problem is that if a customer wants to go to a village that is 50 or 80 km away and that customer shows up at 10:00 pm, it will be late before Syntax gets back, and this makes it difficult to get up in the morning. Sarah says, "He likes to sleep too much," but this is understandable if he has been driving until 11:00 pm or later.

Syntax has his little tricks to keep the day and evening jobs going strong. If I wanted a lift in the morning, he would go to his office and open the door, to make his boss think that he had gone for breakfast. Then he would come and drive me to UB and return to work. He was also careful to be punctual at work when he knew that his boss was writing the annual appraisal of the staff.

Syntax takes his day job very seriously. He dresses well, always wearing a shirt with a matching tie. For the cab driving, he would just wear sweat pants or shorts and a T-shirt. And he would not drive the cab in his shirt and tie except when he snuck out of the office to drive me.

Yes, Syntax took his day job seriously, but not as seriously as he took his football (soccer). On Monday evenings he played on an intramural team. All day Sundays he played with his own neighbourhood teams, which he had organized and financed with money from local businesses to help local youths, he said. This required a lot of organizing, i.e. football meetings on Saturday mornings or on Mondays after intramural football. Football was sacrosanct. Sarah knew that football meetings usually took longer than announced, but she also knew that they were a necessary part of life. Sunday football was the reason that Sarah did not get to go to church very often. Syntax had no objection to babysitting, but not if it meant giving up football.

I never saw Syntax play football, but for a 39-year-old he must have been reasonably good. UB chose him for a staff team that went to Pretoria to play the staff team there. Of course they were royally beaten by Pretoria, but it must have been fun. I was also impressed by the fact that although cell phone airtime was something that Syntax used sparingly — I had to phone him, he wouldn't phone me — he did phone Sarah every night from Pretoria to make sure that everything was OK with her and Jason and Leticia.

> *An anecdote with reflection: Syntax is very attached to his once or twice-daily baths. Here in Canada I once had a text message from him saying that he could not answer the phone because he was bathing. Now I thought that a 39-year-old football player might well feel stiff or sore, and that the bath relieved the sore muscles. Then I saw a newspaper column — by Unity Dow no less — that made fun of Batswana men and their frequent bathing. Her comments reminded me of the many male skin creams and similar cosmetics that were to be found in the local discount supermarket. It seems that in Botswana real men may leave the salad to the goats, but they do use cosmetics.*

Once during August 2009 when Syntax and Sarah were staying with me, Syntax came back from football to find that Sarah had turned off the geyser to save money. (In southern African English a hot water heater is called a geyser.) Syntax was annoyed and dragged my electric kettle out of the cupboard (We were using theirs because it was of better quality.) filled both kettles with water, and plugged them in. The university townhouses are more than twenty-five years old, and the result was predictable. In a minute all the electricity in the house went off, even the television with the soap opera Sarah was watching. Fortunately I knew how to reset the circuit breaker.

Who can say whether Syntax and Sarah are a typical Botswana couple? Perhaps they are not. Neither one has HIV/AIDS. Syntax is a good father and treats Sarah with respect. So I do hope that they are at least representative if not typical. To me they represent Botswana, balancing on the verge of modernity. Every month they struggle to make ends meet and to keep themselves and their children at a level of existence expected in contemporary Botswana. I wish them and their country all the best.

On a personal level I do miss them. They were true friends, as will emerge in other parts of this story. Sometimes I daydream; I imagine what it would be like if they could visit Toronto and see our life here. Jason would love the playground, and Sarah would be fascinated by the dishwasher. They would surely be impressed by the subway and the busy streets. Anyway, this is just a dream. I am sure that they would enjoy such a visit, but it would cost at least $15 000, money that neither they nor I have.

CHAPTER 5   WEDDINGS, FUNERALS, CHURCHES

Weddings and funerals are the principal ceremonies of life in Botswana. Birthdays and christenings just don't cut it in comparison. I was quite jealous when, during my first months in the guest house, several of my expatriate colleagues were invited to these events but no invitation came my way.

Then, in August 2009, the son of one of my colleagues was getting married, and we in the department were all invited. The village of Mochudi, the one from which Alexander McCall Smith's fictional heroine Precious Ramotswe hails, is now a combination of a small town and a suburb. My colleague's family yard is on the outskirts of the town, and since the family was quite prosperous, it was a big yard. When we arrived we were asked to sit on a row of chairs near the gate, where we were served cold drinks. Then the bride arrived. She was greeted by the groom's family with a broom and cooking implements, which symbolized her future duties. A little while later, we were ushered into the main seating area where, under a large tent, a head table and many other ornately dressed tables had been set up. All of us from UB were assigned to two tables near the entrance to the tent.

The bride wore a traditional white wedding gown and the groom a dark suit, and the formalities began with a prayer read by a minister. I learned later that this wedding had been formalized in two parts. The first one, the previous week, had consisted of a church service followed by a celebration in the bride's family yard. Now the second celebration took place in the yard of the groom's family. We were served the best of Botswana food: seswaa (shredded beef) and samp (corn porridge with beans) as well as well as wine and soft drinks. There were also some short speeches. There must have been a religious ceremony that morning, and there was probably dancing later, but since I depended on lifts provided by colleagues, I missed those events.

Wedding customs vary considerably among the various Tswana tribes and regions. The tribe based in Mochudi are the Bakgatla. (I have given them the nickname the Québécois of Botswana. More of that later.) Here I should mention that Bakgatla wedding customs also include an earlier ceremony whereby the groom's friends and relatives visit the bride's family at 6:00 am to formally request the lady's hand. This must have happened at least two weeks before.

There was something unusual about this ceremony that did relate to the Bakgatla's search for a distinctive identity. The groom's father was absent. Why? The Bakgatla have decided to revive the initiation ceremonies which once marked a young man's and a young woman's passage to adulthood. Since these ceremonies had been abandoned for decades, many middle-aged men and women, especially those active in tribal politics, who had missed out on the ceremony in their youth, decided to participate now. What happens during the preparation for these ceremonies is supposed to be top secret, and anyone who reveals anything can be punished by the tribal courts.

The men's ceremony includes spending some days and nights, spread over several weeks, camping out in the bush. It also includes male circumcision, but that is now done in a hospital. The women only spend one night in the bush, just before the end of the initiation. As my friend Keletso, herself a Mokgatla who chose to undergo the initiation, explained, the women are needed at home to do the cooking and cleaning and look after the children. So they cannot be absent for nights on end.

To get back to the wedding, the groom's father showed up halfway through the wedding lunch, dressed in shorts and a large ostrich feather attached to the back of his head. That was a sign that he had successfully completed the initiation. I have a photo of him in his initiation outfit among the wedding guests in their suits and dresses.

Why do I call the Bakgatla the Québécois of Botswana? Because they always seem to be searching for a distinct identity. In 1895, when three Tswana chiefs took their epoch-making trip to England to persuade — successfully — the Colonial Secretary, the famous imperialist Joseph Chamberlain, not to hand the country over to Cecil Rhodes's private company, the Bakgatla chief was asked to come along, but he refused. Another example: The Bakgatla tribal museum in Mochudi displays a letter written by a colonial school inspector who in the 1920s visited schools in the Bechuanaland Protectorate (Botswana's pre-independence name). The letter praises the Bakgatla school for its cleanliness and the good discipline of the children. The inspector contrasts the conditions in the Mochudi school with that in the Bangwato school further north, which he says was dirty and disorganized. The Bangwato are the dominant tribe of the country, the one which produced the first and also the current (the fourth) president. I found this display of praise from the colonial authorities rather pathetic.

And now the Bakgatla have revived initiation ceremonies. Many other Batswana find that practice quaint and vaguely ridiculous. The Bakgatla also seem determined to assert their local autonomy. While I was there, there was controversy over corporal punishment administered to vandals and other petty criminals. The Botswana criminal system does allow corporal (as well as capital) punishment, but the central government claimed that the Bakgatla tribal courts were not giving the accused a fair trial before the punishment was administered. The central government authorities charged the tribal leaders with assault and breaching the constitution. They were imprisoned, but managed to escape, all eleven of them, when they were taken to court. They were recaptured. Eventually the chief was allowed to flee to South Africa (The Bakgatla tribal lands straddle the border.) and the others got off with minor punishments.

(Postscript — In the 2014 election the governing party lost all the seats it had held in the Bakgatla territory; even the popular human rights lawyer and novelist Unity Dow could not win a seat there.)

The groom's father, in shorts and with an ostrich feather on his head, is late for the wedding lunch

Men dancing at a ZCC funeral

I attended two other weddings, one of a colleague, which was unexceptional except for the presence of a live band and the ride back with a second colleague. This man had had a drink or two and was determined to show off his new Mercedes. When we passed some round-faced, dark-skinned people on the road, he made a comment to the effect that he could have run down some of these Zimbabweans but thought better of it. (Batswana usually have oval faces and are somewhat lighter-skinned than the people to the north.)

At every wedding and funeral I attended, I noticed that once the invited guests had eaten their fill, the rest of the village showed up to eat what was left. The women would drape their shoulders in a blue plaid blanket, as a sign of respect for the newly married couple (or the deceased).

The third wedding I attended was that of the son of a well-to-do family in Serowe, the home city of the Bangwato tribe and of the President of the country. Although the family had a perfectly good large yard right in town where they could have held the wedding lunch, they chose to show off by renting a hall from a private school. (This also prevented village hangers-on from dropping by for food after the invited guests had eaten.)

In the morning, there was the church service in an independent fundamentalist church. The church was small and quite crowded. The minister used the old-fashioned terminology by which a wife was instructed to "honour and obey" her husband. This caused a titter from the congregation, behaviour which aroused the ire of the minister who repeated his words with more emphasis.

At the end of the formal ceremony, the minister asked us to give generously because the couple had spent a lot of money on this wedding. Now that was different: a minister asking the guests to contribute to the cost of the wedding.

After the church ceremony, we were instructed to go to the hall after a couple of hours while the couple had their pictures taken. We did so, but there was no sign of the couple. There were ushers, dressed in purple T-shirts printed with the names of the bride and groom. They showed us to our table, but we waited a long time before the couple appeared. The colour theme was white and purple. The bride wore a white dress, of course, and the several bridesmaids were clad in lilac. The couple did a kind of ceremonial dance as they walked through the hall and to the head table. Then we finally received our meal. By this time it was mid-afternoon. We did not stay for most of the speeches and further ceremonies, as we were scheduled to drive further north to the Khama Rhino Sanctuary. Rhinos are almost never seen on the ordinary game drives. So the government has established a game sanctuary for them. (My husband Parkash was on a visit to Botswana at that time; he attended the wedding and went to the rhino sanctuary with me.)

Funerals are a significant part of Tswana life. And I mean that: Funerals are a part of *life*. They are not just occasions for mourning.

Funeral customs vary less from tribe to tribe than do weddings, but there is a significant difference according to the wealth or otherwise of the family. Well-to-do families have funerals that extend over a couple of years. Beginning on the day after the death, there are prayers at the house of the deceased. Friends and family gather in the yard, starting in the late afternoon and continuing until six or seven pm. They chant prayers and sing hymns. At one such prayer session, the singing seemed to consist almost exclusively of these two lines:

> *Modimo fa le teng*
> *Ga yo mathata,*
> (God is with us; our troubles are gone.)

There should be no problem remembering those lines.

At this funeral, we just sat in the yard and sang. At the other, where the daughter of the deceased was a colleague at the University whom I knew quite well, I was asked to come into the house and pay my respect to the deceased as well as to his widow, who sat in the same room as the body.

At prayers, the food served usually consists of tea and cookies. However, when her father died, my colleague decided to serve juice with small scones which she had baked herself. That was a considerable undertaking because her father was a retired police chief, and the prayers were attended by forty or fifty policemen, active and retired, as well as, of course, relatives and colleagues from UB. The yard was packed with folding chairs, and people seemed to be coming and going all the time.

After the public prayers, there is an all-night vigil of prayers for the family. This is done to comfort the family of the deceased, and also bid the deceased farewell and ask that his/her journey to heaven be smooth.

Early on the Saturday morning following the death, there is the funeral itself. A couple of years later, for those who can afford it, there is the unveiling of the tombstone. Both occasions call for further ceremonies.

My first "funeral" was a tombstone unveiling in a village south of Gaborone. My colleague Gladys had offered me a lift, but that morning her car broke down, and by the time her brother managed to make it roadworthy, we were very late. We drove to the cemetery, which we had difficulty finding, and there we found the tombstone already unveiled. There were only a couple of prayers and hymns left to sing.

We drove back to the family yard, where there were speeches, including one from the head of the local village council who wore a white suit. The speeches were in Setswana. After the speeches, lunch was served. The women of the family had stayed behind to prepare the meal, and the food was really good, probably the best Botswana food I had during my time there.

The next tombstone unveiling took place in Serowe. My housemate Wynie and I asked Syntax to drive us to this pleasant town about 400 km north of Gaborone. We stayed in a guest house right next to the yard of the family where the ceremonies were to take place. In the morning we walked over to the yard, where a religious service was held and members of the family made speeches. This is the only time that I saw any display of sadness at a funeral or related event. The youngest son in the family, who had tried to look after and help his older brother before alcoholism killed him two years previously, was obviously still much affected by his brother's death.

The family spared no expense in organizing the ceremonies. There was a program of several pages, printed in colour on glossy paper, with pictures of the deceased and witty sayings attributed to him. He must have been a *bon vivant* who really enjoyed life — until his lifestyle killed him. I noticed an interesting aspect of the hymn singing. To accommodate those who might not be able to read, a woman read out each line before it was time to sing it.

After the service, we drove and marched to the cemetery for the unveiling of the tombstone, where there were more prayers and hymns. I looked around at the tombstones and more modest grave markers and noticed how many people had died in their twenties and thirties during the early 2000s, at the height of the HIV/AIDS epidemic. I also noticed, as Syntax had told me, that many families could not afford tombstones. Instead, the graves consisted of a low mound of earth, surrounded by a low green wire fence to which a simple sign with the name and date of birth and death had been attached.

After the unveiling there was the obligatory lunch in the family yard, but with a difference. There were two tables with tubs of hot food. I stood in the shorter line, but was quickly chased away by my Canadian friend Tom (who lived in Serowe). He pointed out that there was a men's line and a women's line, and I was in the wrong one. Apparently, I had lined up for a ceremonial dish (*mokoto*) that only men are allowed to eat and whose composition is kept secret. (I believe that it was made of the innards of a game animal. Perhaps I wasn't missing much.)

By September 2012 I had attended two tombstone unveilings but no real funeral. Of course I could not wish someone dead to create a funeral for me, but one day I did mention to one of the university librarians that I had not yet had a chance to attend a Tswana funeral. A couple of weeks later she got back to me. The mother of the inter-library loan librarian had died, and the other librarians had booked a combi to take them to the village where the funeral would take place. There was a seat left in the rental combi, and if I was willing to pay 100P for my share of the cost, I was in.

Funerals always begin about 6:00 am, usually on a Saturday. This village was in the Palapye area. We had to leave at 3:00 am to arrive on time. I caught a couple of hours sleep in my funeral clothes, and my librarian friend picked me up and drove me to the combi pickup point. Some people were late, of course, and we did not leave until 3:30. It was the coldest time of the night, and my female colleagues were dressed in many layers of clothing and wrapped in blankets. Inside the combi, I got one of those seats on the edge near the aisle where I was in constant danger of slipping off. Nevertheless I fell fast asleep as soon as I sat down. Around 5:30, just as the sun was coming up, we stopped at a well-equipped roadside stop for tea. I noticed that the bathrooms were clean and well equipped. They even had that scarce Botswana item, toilet paper (See Chapter 8.)

By the time we got back into the combi, it was almost 6:00. The driver had some difficulty finding the village — in Botswana the roads are good, but there are few road signs — so that by the time we got to the village and found the right yard, it was quarter to seven and the funeral was already in progress. First we were asked to walk through the house to see the body of the deceased. Then we went out to the yard and sat on folding chairs. There were no programs left, but someone let me see one. It was written entirely in Setswana, but I managed to learn that the deceased was 56 years old and had had five children.

There was some singing of hymns out in the yard, but there was also a group of maybe ten men in beige uniforms who were doing a kind of circle dance with their backs to us in the space between the chairs and the wall of the house. Some women also danced. Between 8:00 and 9:00 am we all got into cars and drove to the cemetery for the burial. The men in beige uniforms were there and stood around the open grave in a circle. As the minister preached, he lifted his hands from time to time and the men in beige all jumped in unison.

I learned later that the deceased's family belonged to the ZCC (Zionist Christian Church), which is based in South Africa but also has many adherents in Botswana. Although they do not encourage outsiders to visit their services, these apparently include dancing and levitation. Hence the dancing at the funeral.

At the cemetery, I stood toward the back of the crowd. In order to see better, I climbed onto a little mound of earth. Someone immediately pushed me away. These mounds of earth, not even surrounded by a fence, were poor people's graves. Two graves caught my attention. Someone had attempted to surround one grave with small rocks, a good idea if you could not afford even a little wire fence, but whoever it was had been interrupted, so that the stones only extended around two sides of the grave. Then there was a small grave, obviously a child's. It was only marked by a mound of earth on the top of which there lay a headless, naked Barbie doll.

After a service of about an hour, we returned to the family yard. We city folks were separated from the others and asked to sit in a kind of barn in which chairs had been placed for us. Instead of serving ourselves from the communal tubs, we were brought plates of food. I noticed that the female relatives who were performing this task spoke to each other in a language that was not Setswana. I was tired from lack of sleep, the air was getting hot, and I was suddenly possessed by a surreal feeling that I was in a strange place, that the whole scene around me was somehow not real and that I was accompanying an explorer in nineteenth century Africa.

I snapped out of it when someone handed me a plate of food consisting of seswaa, samp and corn porridge. The first thing I had to do was ask for a fork or spoon. We were expected to use our corn porridge to pick up the food, a skill I did not have. I tried to eat the food, but it was so absolutely awful that I could not. I went to the large open door of the barn where a few skinny dogs had gathered and tipped my plate in front of them. The first dog ate only the seswaa; then the second dog ate the two porridges.

I learned later that we were in a Batswapong village, the tribe to which Syntax and Sarah belong. This group emigrated from South Africa within the last two centuries and lives in several villages in the Bangwato area. Their dialect is related to Setswana, but as it does not have books or a literature, its future is uncertain. The

British did not recognize the Batswapong as a separate tribe, and the present government does not do so either. Batswapong villages have their own local government, but there is not a tribal government as such. While I was there, there was a long and drawn out controversy about the reorganization of four village governments in the area where the Batswapong live.

The largest village, Seleka, was determined to maintain its autonomy-my, while the government wanted to create a new mega-village. When the government put up road signs with the new name of the mega-village, someone defaced the signs and wrote Seleka across the new name. (Shades of Mike Harris's megacity?) But when the national census was held in 2011, it was the other three villages who complained and refused to be listed as part of the mega-village. They wanted to show that their combined population was greater than that of Seleka. No one went to jail or was fined for refusing to participate in the census. Government officials worked out a compromise.

That was my first Botswana funeral. The second and last one was that of Gladys's father, as mentioned above. It was routine and uneventful, or rather I knew the routine by then. And since Gladys's family belonged to a regular church, there was no dancing and jumping around.

On a related subject, I had read somewhere that Botswana has mainline churches (such as Catholics and Anglicans), fundamentalist churches, and African-type churches that combined Christian theology with African ritual. I immediately decided that I needed to visit an African church. I spent much time and money, and other peoples' time as well, trying to find an African church. The guy from the local internet café took me to his church, which met in a hut made of sheets of aluminium sheeting in the suburb of Tlokweng. The small congregation was extremely nice to me, finding me a bilingual New Testament so that I could follow the service. In that church, as in many others, the initiates wore a uniform, in this case, white and blue shirts for the men, dresses with white collars for the women. That Sunday there was a ceremony in which some young men were initiated into the church, a lengthy ceremony involving the sprinkling of water.

A former student, Tebogo, invited me to her church. They did not have their own building but met in a hall rented from a private college. This church concentrated on doing good works; the current project was building a house for a poor family. After the service, the parishioners served apple juice and cookies, and the service was of a normal length, not exceptionally long as the one in Tlokweng had been.

One of the social work professors at the University was rumoured to be a traditional "medicine man". He was active in a church in a nearby village. I figured that that had to be a real African church. I asked him the time of the service, and on the next Sunday, while Syntax was playing football, Sarah (accompanied by Jason) drove me to the village. We both attended the service, and Jason was good and sat still for most the hour and a half or so. This service included a lot of music; the social work professor played a wind instrument but otherwise there was nothing exceptional about the service. Jason had been so good that I treated him to an ice cream on the way back.

My friend and colleague Keb said he would help me find a true African church. Somewhere, I had conceived the idea that a true African church would have the word apostolic in its title. With the help of the internet (really!) I found a church, St. Paul's, in a relatively poor neighbourhood in central Gaborone, not far from where Syntax and Sarah lived. The following Sunday, Keb and I set out for that church. The church consisted a of a simple building — I think it was made of wood — and inside there was quite a large congregation, of perhaps 60–70, with all the women on one side, the men on the other. Keb went to sit with the men, but I was given a special seat near the door, near but not with the other women. It was a long service, consisting of various prayers, preaching and hymn singing. There was nothing exceptional about the service. The uniform for that church was similar to that I had seen in Tlokweng, white and blue. It was very hot in the building, but water was available. Finally, after more than two hours, Keb and I decided to leave. I called Sarah to come and pick us up. When we left, I looked at the sign on the gate post. It said, "St. Peter's Apostolic Church".

After that experience, I decided that my initial information about a distinct category of African Christian churches might have been wrong. What there is in Botswana is a large variety of fundamentalist Christian churches. Many of them are independent, one-person shows started by a single preacher who somehow managed to attract followers. It was a good living if a person could attract disciples with his/her preaching. It provided an even better living if you already had a day job. The university housing manager, for example, was the minister of a church in a town about forty kilometres south of Gaborone.

While many of the churches were stand-alone, others were affiliated with mother churches in South Africa. The government of Botswana was concerned that these churches were extracting money from Batswana, money which then left the country. While I was there, the government, in an attempt to prevent fraud and abuse, required all churches to submit annual audited financial statements. This was not a big problem for the traditional denominations. A trip to Africa in return for doing the audit was a nice perk for retired accountants from the US, the UK or Finland. (The Lutheran churches in Botswana have links to those in Finland.) The smaller local churches had to scramble to find the money to pay an auditor.

From time to time, large posters appeared on the walls of the University, downtown and at combi stops advertising visits by itinerant preachers from South Africa. Some of these claimed to be healers as well. I never had the nerve to attend one of these events.

Gospel music is very popular. I attended a concert by a famous South African gospel singer. The hall was a cavernous agricultural exhibition hall, not well suited to the purpose, but the people in the audience (which was not all that numerous, considering the size of the hall) seemed to be enjoying the show. One not-very-young lady of traditional stature stood on her chair, singing along. There were a number of young ladies with those plunging, reveal-the-cleavage necklines that President Khama objects to.

Botswana also has the traditional mainline churches. Catholics, Lutherans, Baptists, Anglicans, Seventh-day Adventists and Methodists all have more than one church and congregation in Gaborone. There is a distinct class system at work here. Poor people tend to belong to the local fundamentalist churches, which operate on the McDonald's principle of small amounts of money from many people. The uniforms must also be quite an expense for a maid or supermarket cashier who only earns a pittance, but people are happy to earn the right to wear these uniforms as they rise through the ranks of the initiated.

The ZCC or Zionist Christian Church is a large church, based in South Africa, and it has taken the idea of creating a sense of belonging further than any other of the local churches. Ideally it wants men to wear beige outfits and women long skirts and a kind of turban. It also forbids the consumption of pork, caffeine and alcohol. But the uniforms the church requires are not always practical. A store clerk needs to wear practical clothes or perhaps a store uniform. So those who cannot follow the required dress code at all times wear a large silver-coloured star, like a Star of David attached to their clothing. I saw many of those stars when shopping. My assigned driver at the Botswana Defence Force wore the star on his military uniform.

An interesting example of the class nature of Botswana's religions: Bayapo, the girl who stayed with me while preparing for her exams, belonged to the ZCC church. I asked her to allow me to accompany her to one of the services. She demurred, saying that I needed to cover my head and wear a long skirt. I said that I could easily do that, having attended services in Sikh temples where similar conditions apply. But she still would not take me along. She probably thought I would not be impressed by levitation or in-service dances, though I surely could have coped.

Bayapo has now graduated from UB, and though she could not find a job as a teacher, her chosen profession, she did get a good job with an NGO. She now flies to Johannesburg instead of going there in combis, the cheapest means of transport. She has also left the ZCC, changed her name, including the spelling of her first name (I have used the old name here to protect her identity.), and she eats pork and drinks tea.

Botswana is a profoundly Christian nation. There is no concept of the separation of church and state. Local people are expected to be Christians. When I attended a dinner of the association of police officers, it began not with the national anthem, but a prayer. Ditto for wedding receptions. At the beginning of the exam period, the University holds a prayer session which students can attend to pray for success in the exams. The BDF officers who studied at UB had a packed program, which included physical exercises, so that they would not become slack while they were studying, but it also included a half-hour prayer service on Monday mornings. In September and October, the village councils (*dikgotla*) hold prayers in which they ask for rain during the upcoming spring and summer.

According to the *CIA World Factbook*, Botswana is 72% Christian, and 6% "Badimo", which presumably means traditional religions. (The word *badimo* means gods.) I did not meet anyone who said that s/he followed a traditional religion, but I did not travel to remote villages. My neighbours were both professors, and their teenaged daughter was a very troubled person. She drank, smoked and stole. Her parents tried everything, including a strict, expensive Catholic boarding school. Finally they sent her to the father's home village in the north of the country, where the grandfather wanted to subject her to a traditional ceremony that would purge her of her problems. The parents were willing to allow this, but the girl refused. And I only have this story from the girl herself, not the most reliable source (though in this case the parents can perhaps not be blamed for being willing to try anything). Unity Dow's book *Saturday is for Funerals* (Harvard University Press, 2010) includes the sad story of a maid who paid a whole month's earnings to a traditional medicine man who promised to cure her brother of AIDS.

Background fact: Traditional healers in Botswana apparently engage in some particularly pernicious practices. At a seminar on maternal mortality, I heard that village midwives encourage bleeding by post-partum women because they believe that there is nine months' worth of blood that needs to come out. I wonder how many women that practice has killed?

According to the Indian High Commissioner, there are seven Hindu temples in the country as well as one Sikh gurudwara. The temples include one of the Hare Krishna sect who try to convert local people to Hinduism. I attended one of their functions, where local teenagers were acting in skits based on the Bhagavad Gita. There are also a number of mosques, though no one seems to know how many; I was told four or five. There is a mosque across the street from the main entrance to the University. In front of it there stands a large green and yellow sign:

>WELCOME TO
>ISLAM
>WELCOMES YOU.

The government has worried about the possibility of Islamic extremists coming in from other African countries. Nigerian professors have apparently been finding it difficult to obtain or renew visas.

There are also about 50 000 Chinese in Botswana, but they do not follow any religion, as far as anyone can tell. There are no Buddhist or any other Chinese temples.

Taking all of the above into consideration, I believe the number of 72% Christians to be an underestimate. Many people go to church every week; many more are affiliated with a church, though they may not attend regularly. Of the many local people I met, I can remember only one, my driver Syntax, who admitted not belonging to any church; he said that he could be a good Christian and good person without belonging to any church. Amen to that.

CHAPTER 6   CRIME — AND PUNISHMENT?

When people think of going to Africa, they usually expect to find a fair amount of crime wherever they might travel. It is certainly an impression most of us have of South Africa. Many of us have heard of the honeymoon murder in Cape Town and the Oscar Pistorius trial and high crime rates generally. We think of Nigeria and Kenya as hotbeds of crime, and as for the Democratic Republic of the Congo and Somalia, to mention only two countries, the concept of law and order would appear to be only a distant fantasy, a *fata morgana*. A friend of mine who is an old Africa hand, having lived in two Portuguese-speaking African countries, was visiting me. She was shocked when she saw me wearing a little gold-plated necklace. "You're not going out wearing that," she said one morning, thinking that someone might attack me for my jewellery. I assured her that I had worn that and other necklaces since I came to Botswana, and nothing had ever happened to me.

As a Botswana booster, I like to pooh-pooh those who ask me about crime. After all, I seldom felt threatened (See the chapter on transport.) or afraid. But now with hindsight, I must admit that over my three years there, I did experience some crime.

Let me try to get a perspective on things by remembering times when I was a victim of crime in Canada, which means that I am not counting the time when my purse was stolen in Germany (1990), my wallet in a French laundromat (1991), or my hand luggage in a railway station in Venezuela (1989) and in another railway station in Milan (1998). As far as I can remember, my first experience of crime was when someone stole my purse at a bus stop in Vancouver in 1961 or so. I had one of those clutch purses that were popular at the time; I had left it lying next to me on the bench at a bus stop while I was reading. Wasn't that almost asking someone to take it?

When we lived in Sudbury, Ontario, thieves entered our house twice, but on both occasions we had left the door open. On the first occasion, they took some spare change from the children's piggy banks, but also helped themselves to a diamond necklace my husband had given me for our 25th wedding anniversary. The thieves must have entered our house, but we did not even realize anything was missing until I came home one day and encountered a teenager running out of the house. And the police did recover the necklace. On the second occasion, someone walked into our house on a cold winter evening and helped her/himself to our brand-new VCR player. We never recovered it, and it seems that the person did not want anything else. Also in Sudbury, someone took my wallet out of the purse in my office at Laurentian University. Later a colleague found it in a men's washroom, without the cash but everything else intact. I had left the office wide open, and, that according to the police, was the way some people supported themselves. On a Friday afternoon, they would go through the University and the nursing stations in the nearby hospital and help themselves to the cash that people had taken out of the bank for the weekend.

We haven't ever been the victims of crime since we moved to Toronto, perhaps because we have been more careful and locked our house when we go out, except perhaps for a few minutes to run to the corner store to buy vegetables. No, on second thought I lie. My wallet was emptied once at a Christmas party organized by the Liberal Party in the University of Toronto area. Apart from that, we have not been the victims of crime by strangers.

Unfortunately, as nephews and nieces grew up, in-house crime became quite common. Two nieces shared an apartment in our city. Their idea of furnishing their apartment with household utensils and items such as toilet paper or shampoo was to help themselves to things from our house. It was not as if they would ask, "Auntie, would you mind lending me a roll of toilet paper?" No, the stuff just disappeared after they came for a friendly visit. It was our son Paul who was most observant here. He would check the toilet paper holder in the bathroom when one of them had left. And it was he who noticed the absence of my best French-language dictionary. That was not too hard to track down. We knew who was studying French. Eventually at least one of the nieces and later a nephew graduated to helping him/herself to cash from my purse, so that we had to take appropriate precautions when they were around. Fortunately it would appear that all three of them have now grown up to be responsible citizens. But does within-the-family crime count?

The above are offered by way of background for my experiences in Botswana.

In January 2009, a friend from Canada and our son Paul's now ex-wife were visiting Botswana. We all decided to go out for Chinese food and came back less than two hours later. When we came back, the contents of some of our suitcases were strewn all over the landing on the stairs leading to the second floor, and my laptop was lying on the living room floor. A little further investigation revealed that someone had broken the backdoor lock to enter the house. The thieves were discerning. They only took cash and gold jewellery, and there had not been very much of either. I was happy to keep my laptop and all the data therein, but its presence on the living room floor was a bit of a mystery. Perhaps we had interrupted the intruders, and they dropped the laptop as we arrived. Or maybe a three-year-old Toshiba was not good enough for them.

We called the police and then asked Syntax, who had just dropped us off, to come back and give us advice. He came immediately, and we sat around the dining room table and waited for the police to arrive. We had come home around 8:00 pm. At 9:00, no sign of the police. By 10:00, Syntax was beginning to look very tired. I plied him with cake and coffee. By eleven o'clock, still no sign of the police. Parkash and Syntax decided to drive to the main downtown police station to check on what was happening. The police station was about two kilometres away. When they had driven about half the way, they encountered a group of four policemen, walking with their tall rifles in hand. They were walking to my place! They had waited for transport, and when no car became available, and we phoned to ask where they were, they decided to walk. Since Syntax could not take them all in his car, they continued the walk to my house, where they arrived before midnight.

They did the usual, asking us questions, filling out forms and asking us to come to the police station the next day to sign more documents. They also took fingerprints of the backdoor. I suspected that not much would come of this investigation, and I was right, though our American friend Chandni, who worked for an NGO in downtown Gaborone, told me that when someone stole the safe from their office, the police took fingerprints and actually caught someone.

In the meanwhile, Paul and Raman had done a bit of their own detective work. It had been raining that evening, and there were footprints in the soil in the backyard. They led from and to the fence separating my yard from that of House 27, occupied by a Tanzanian professor of statistics. The fence was almost five feet high, so not that easy to jump over, but it seems that the designers of the complex wanted to encourage friendly neighbourly relations. So they had scooped a semi-circular shape out of the concrete wall, a spot where neighbours could meet and chat. At that point, the wall was only about two feet high and quite easy to cross. On the other side of House 27, between it and house 26, there was a footpath which led from the street to the Botswana Telecommunications Authority property behind the houses. It, of course, was surrounded by a high fence topped with barbed wire and with plenty of security guards lurking about.

The next day I talked to the professor in the neighbouring House 27 and asked him if he had heard or seen anything. He was quite offended and seemed to think that I was accusing him of allowing the thief to pass through his yard. He insisted that it was impossible for any intruder to cross his yard, that he had a fierce dog that the intruder(s) would have encountered if they tried to cross his yard. But the footprint evidence was there.... The neighbour was never very friendly after that, but, of course, I absolutely did not suspect him or his family.

As for the fierce dog, he did bark loudly whenever I had visitors and really frightened Jason, but he soon got used to me, especially after I started throwing him bits of leftovers.

The maid Nora had been cleaning the house that day, and as she was a Zimbabwean, people told me that she might have tipped someone off that we would not be home. I did not think so at the time, but if you have read about Nora in Chapter 2, you may think differently.

Also during that month of January 2009, I went to an academic conference in Mauritius. Parkash and Paul came to Johannesburg with me, where we stayed in the lovely Balalaika Hotel. At that time the hotel was attached to a small mall, which included an ATM of the FNB bank, the one with which I banked in Gaborone. I can never resist an ATM of my bank. It is a bit like a wolf marking his territory. So I went to the mall and withdrew some South African rands. There were two men behind me, and one of them stood very close. When I asked him to move back, he said he wanted to see if I needed any help, which of course I did not.

When I returned from Mauritius four days later and went to take money from the ATM in Gaborone, my bank account had shrunk by about 20 000 pula (almost $3000 Canadian). A printout from the bank confirmed that someone in South Africa had withdrawn money from my account in transactions of one thousand rand at a time. The bank's first reaction was that if I went through the proper motions, it would refund the money. So I filled out many forms, and Parkash and I went to the local magistrate's office to fill out an affidavit and submit it to the bank. I decided on a strategy of visiting the bank twice a week, to remind them that I was waiting for my money.

After about a week, the bank changed its tune. The staff told me that since the money was stolen from an ATM and not in a store, I was not entitled to a refund. On the wall of the bank, there was a helpful chart which detailed how FNB dealt with customer complaints. Complaints went from the branch manager up to a regional manager and finally to a central complaints department in South Africa. I decided to work my way up the pyramid while continuing my visits to the branch until someone gave my money back.

About two weeks after the thefts, I arrived at the bank for one of my regular visits. An employee greeted me with, "Professor Mahant, we have good news for you." Great, I thought, they will refund my money. No, not at all. The good news was that the bank had checked the machine in the Balalaika Hotel and had found a magnetic reader — seventeen days after I reported the problem. I did not know whether to laugh or cry. The distance from Gaborone to Johannesburg is 400 km, and the communication facilities linking the two cities are good. Several flights per day take about 45 minutes to make the trip; a private car can make it in five hours or less, including the border crossing; a bus takes seven hours, because it needs more time to cross the border. Internet and telephone connections are also excellent between these two major centres. And it had taken the bank two and a half weeks to check the ATM? I finally retorted, "I could walk to Johannesburg in seventeen days."

I left and went home to my faithful laptop and started to write one of my letters to the manager of the bank. I pointed out that many people must have lost money while that magnetic reader was still in the machine in Sandton. Why had no one phoned the nearest FNB branch and asked them to check that ATM immediately? How much more money had been stolen during those seventeen days? I hand-delivered the letter the next day, and continued my visits to the bank. A few days later the manager asked to speak with me. He asked me to write the branch a letter in which I would thank them for their good service; in return the bank would refund the stolen money, all except the fees the thieves had accumulated while making their withdrawals. (Was it not Henry IV of France who said, as he converted to Catholicism, "Paris is worth a Mass"? If so, a false letter of appreciation is worth 20 000 pula.) I wrote the letter, being careful not to be too fulsome in my praise. I had good relations with the branch for the rest of my time in Botswana.

My further brushes with crime in Botswana were less dramatic but also had less successful outcomes. One of the teaching assistants, someone with whom I was quite friendly, asked to borrow some money to start a business. I think it was 4000 pula. I hesitated but finally gave him the money. He used it to start an advertising business, printing flyers that would become newspaper inserts. His business did well, and a couple of months later he returned all of the money. I put it in a plain brown envelope in my desk drawer, covered it with some other papers, and for the next couple of weeks used the money as a source of cash instead of lining up at an ATM. Then, one day when I went to the drawer to get some money, the envelope was gone. No one except the cleaning staff had access to that office, and they were so nice and friendly. Someone must have rifled through the office to find the money. There was no way anyone could have known the money was there, because I reached for it only when I was alone. Even if I had left the office open for a minute or two during the day, no one would have had time to rifle through my papers and find the money. So whoever did it must have been doing regular searches through various offices.

That apparently did happen. A colleague told me how he had sold tickets for some event at his children's private school and kept the money in his desk drawer. It all disappeared, and he had to make up the loss.

My neighbour's daughter looked and acted like a teenager, and she did attend high school with other teenagers, but she was in fact twenty-one years old. She had missed two years of school when she was sixteen and ran away with a gang of cell phone thieves. At the time I am writing about, October and November 2012, her mother and younger brother were away in Australia while the mother, a professor, was on sabbatical. One day the girl asked me if I could help her study for an English literature test. I like literature, and I was attracted by the idea of an insight into the local school system. So I agreed.

Helping her soon became a commitment. She started bringing homework for other subjects, and she ate her way through much of the food in my fridge. She said that she liked the European-style food I bought much better than what her father bought. OK, but the South African items I had were of course more expensive than the local food. She also started complaining how badly her father treated her, not letting her stay out all night at her age. Well, yes, but she had a history, as I mentioned earlier. She had a drinking problem and smoked when she could, maybe not just nicotine. But she also told me that she did not like children, and unlike many young women her age, she had not produced any babies.

In November 2012, I started to notice that money was missing from my purse. I did not want trouble with my neighbour, a university administrator, nor did I want to bother the girl's mother, who was on sabbatical. So I took the precaution of putting my purse in the bedroom whenever the girl came over. But money was still disappearing. I was mystified. I lived in a two-storey house, and my pupil had no reason to go upstairs, and in fact I never saw her go there. So how did she manage to get at my money? Or were the cleaning staff at the University getting so bold that they were taking money from my locked office while I was in class? I am notoriously careless about exactly how much I have in my purse, but I did begin to count my cash at various times of the day, and yes, it seemed that money was disappearing during the evenings, when I was at home and M. came for her lessons.

But how did she get the money from the upstairs bedroom? The staircase to the upstairs ran along one wall of the living room, and when I ate, I normally sat on the couch with my back to the staircase, which gave me a good view of the television. Did I mention that my no-longer-teenaged friend also liked to watch soap operas while she studied?

One evening, she offered to make me a cup of tea while I was trying to explicate a poem by a lesser-known Elizabethan poet. This was not unusual. We often had tea together. But that evening, for some reason, I chose to sit on the other side of the living room as I struggled to find some meaning in the poem. The other side meant that I was facing the stairway instead of having my back to it.

My young friend came back with the tea, and as she served to me, she asked me why I was sitting on that side of the living room. That was when the penny dropped. She must have been sneaking upstairs while I had my back to the stairs and making quick trips into the bedroom to take money from my purse. The noise from the television ensured that I did not hear her go up and down the stairs.

So I sadly had to repeat the manoeuvre of putting an exact amount of money in my purse etc., as I had done with Nora two years earlier. When I was sure who was taking the money, I made an appointment with her father at the University and told him the sad story. He did not seem upset. Basically he said something like: There she goes again. He offered to pay me back the money, but since I had no idea how much had gone missing over the months, I refused the offer.

When the mother returned from Australia a couple of weeks later, she was horrified and tried to make things up to me by taking me for a last-minute shopping trip to a lovely little mall where various small shops sold mostly African souvenirs and where she also bought me lunch in an Italian restaurant.

> *Sequel:* M. did very well in her final exams. Her grades were good enough to go to the University of Botswana, but she chose to go to a private business college, where she is studying accounting (not creative accounting, I hope). M. had taken business courses in high school as she dreamt of starting her own business. Her mother reports that her studies are going well – but she must have been pregnant by the time she started her studies. She produced a baby just after her final exams after the first year, in April 2014. Her parents could have taken her the 15 km across the border to South Africa for an abortion, but that is not the Tswana way. The mother will now be a babysitting grandmother as well as a full-time professor while M. completes her studies. The family also brought a teenaged cousin from a village to attend school in Gaborone and help with the extra work of looking after little Leila. Now that is the Tswana way.

That is about it for crime which I experienced myself. And I can't say that many friends experienced crimes while I was there. One exception was Bayapo who lived in a row of single rooms in a nearby village which had become a suburb. Someone broke into her room while she was away with her family over Christmas and stole her television and her food. Those rooms, where some of the taxi drivers also lived, were apparently subject to break-ins. Of course, better-off people had security systems (I bought one after my break-in.) or fierce-sounding dogs.

But wait; there's more.

One Saturday, I took the crosstown combi to go to a mall at the southern end of the city, the one where the fictional heroine Precious Ramotswe and her secretary friend went to buy blue shoes. As the combi passed through an industrial area, it suddenly jolted to a halt, throwing all of us out of our seats. There was a lot of noise and confusion as the passengers descended from the combi. I asked the young, already-of-traditional-stature woman in blue jeans who had been sitting next to me what was going on. She explained that several passengers in the combi had observed a purse-snatching. The combi stopped and some of the passengers set off in pursuit of the thief.

That struck me as a rather futile enterprise, since the thief obviously had a considerable head start. Still the combi crowd did its best. Some climbed on top of a shed and started shouting out the location of the thief who was still visible, running away with his booty. The thief had bad luck. One of the passengers was a track star, trained in running. He caught the miscreant. There was some more noise and confusion. The thief and some of the passengers appeared across the street from the combi, where there was more shouting and confusion. The road was wide, and I could not see what was going on.

After some minutes, the passengers reassembled and started to climb back into the combi. My interpreter returned from the other side of the road where she had gathered with a small crowd. She had removed the belt that held her blue jeans up and proceeded to reinsert it after she got back into the vehicle. I asked her why she had taken off her belt.

"Oh," she said. "To beat the thief, and he said 'ouch' when I hit him." I asked her if they had called the police. She said that she did not know what had happened. They had given him a good thrashing, and that was enough from her point of view.

An association of colleges in the American Midwest has an arrangement with the University of Botswana whereby a professor with a whole class of students spends a term at the University in Gaborone. One year it was a group of archaeology students, the next year biologists. The professor stayed in whatever accommodation s/he could find (in this case that was my house), but the students were expected to live in the residences with the local students. The American students were thoroughly briefed, told not to go out in the dark, and to avoid local pubs. Of course they did nothing of the sort.

One evening three boys went to a pub and then started to walk home. They were accosted by a group who demanded their money, their phones and their shoes. An altercation ensued, and one of the Americans suffered a small cut, which caused much agonizing on the part of the professor because she feared what the parents back in the US would say if one of her charges contracted HIV/AIDS. Luckily nothing like this happened, so that this part of the story ended well.

So did another part. The boys handed over their shoes, phones and money, but then they pleaded for the return of their shoes as the road was unpaved and they could not walk on it barefoot without great discomfort. The thieves returned the shoes but kept the phones and the money. Those attackers must have been Batswana. Zimbabwean thieves surely would not have been so considerate.

Botswana does have a high crime rate. The murder rate is particularly high and drunk driving is a major problem. Draconian punishments and widespread government propaganda seem to have made little difference. Yet, as I hope I have demonstrated, I did not live in fear or take excessive precautions. I felt quite safe walking around the university campus in the dark, though some parts were very poorly lit. When I stayed in the guest house I regularly walked the one block to and from the Alliance française in the evenings. The road was brightly lit, and the University was nearby. After I moved into my house, I was just a short half block and a bit from the nearest supermarket, and I went there in the evenings without any fear. The canteen where all the policemen in town came to eat was right across from the supermarket. It would have taken a foolhardy criminal to attempt anything there. Around the back of the supermarket, there was a small strip mall which included an excellent internet café where the computers were as fast or faster than they were at the University. Sometimes I went there after work, and in August and September, when the days were very short, I had to walk through a patch of total darkness on the side of the supermarket. As this was somewhat scary, I tried to remember to bring a flashlight or use my phone as a flashlight, but I did not always bother. I found climbing over the log that separated the parking lot of the supermarket from that of the other mall to be scarier than any of the people whom I encountered there.

Yes, I encountered crime in Botswana, but unlike some northerners who stayed there, I did not live in constant fear.

And now for a few more comments and interesting stories about crime in Botswana. Just as the people of Hong Kong blame migrants from the mainland for most of the crime in the territory, Batswana like to blame immigrants and refugees from Zimbabwe for much of the crime that happens in their country. I have not seen any statistics to back up this claim, but there are many Zimbabweans in Botswana's jails.

The Zimbabweans are not the only foreigners who commit crimes. Surprisingly, at least to me, the Chinese — many of whom are not permanent residents of Botswana — also get into trouble with the law. Then I read Paul Theroux's book about his travels in Angola (*The Last Train to Zona Verde*. Houghton Mifflin, 2013). He claims that the Chinese government uses prisoners from Chinese jails when they need manual labourers for their projects in Africa. That certainly would explain high crime rates, if such there are.

A friend of mine who works in the court system told me that many Chinese residents who appear in court have committed "ordinary" crimes, not just the corruption for which the Chinese are well known (and with which Botswana has not dealt effectively). These people claim not to speak English, which means that the Botswana courts have to spend money to hire Mandarin-to-English interpreters. The friend told me a pathetic story of a love triangle. A Chinese woman married to a Chinese man was having an affair with another, younger Chinese man. The three of them decided to meet at Gaborone's only five-star hotel to talk things over. A fight ensued and the younger man beat the older one so badly that he ended up in a wheelchair. Now the local court (near my house) was hearing the assault trial.

(Much has been said and written about the Chinese, who have been denounced as the new colonialists in Africa. It is not a topic I can cover here, but let me note that many Chinese firms are active in Botswana, especially in the construction industry).

Botswana, like many other countries including Canada, has the problem of trigger-happy policemen. In the papers I read a sad story about several policemen who had tortured a suspect during interrogation; the suspect had died, and the police tried to cover their tracks by hanging the body from a tree and claiming that the man had committed suicide. (I have referred to policemen as if they were all male, which is not the case, though those involved in criminal investigations are in fact mostly men. The night the police drove me home from the combi stop — see Chapter 3 — some of those in the vehicle were women. And there are many policewomen patrolling the streets.)

Botswana has a small Greek community, so small that they have intermarried with the local population and so small that the country does not even have one Greek restaurant (though I was under the impression that it only takes one Greek family to start a restaurant). In the Gaborone spring, an elderly Greek couple sold flowers and herb plants off the back of a van outside the Riverwalk mall. In October, the month of the Greek national holiday, the Greeks held a fancy dinner at the five-star hotel on the western outskirts of the city. I did not manage to attend any of these dinners. The price was 400P, and on top of that I would have had to pay a cab to take me there and back.

One year our department at UB had a teaching assistant who was fair-skinned, had a Greek surname but a Setswana first name, and spoke Setswana like a local. Of course I asked her how she came by the Greek surname. She said that her grandfather had been from Greece, had married a local woman and moved to her village and raised a family there. In old age he abandoned his Tswana family and returned to Greece. One of his children was our TA's father. Except for the name, the family was totally integrated into the local community. Our TA spoke Setswana and had attended the local government schools. She was not just of traditional stature: she was obese, and she was given to wearing dresses or blouses that barely covered her ample bosom. I was sure that one day one of her breasts would pop out of that inadequate covering, but it did not happen, at least not while I was in the TA's office.

Gentle reader, you may think that I digress, that all this talk about the Greek community is not about crime, but wait, the most intriguing is yet to come.

John Kalafatis was the son of a well-to-do local family, one of those mixed Greek and local families. John had fallen into bad company. He was involved in the drug trade and had had several brushes with the law. In May 2009 there was a break-in at a home in the wealthy suburb of Phakalane. It would appear that John was one of the burglars, though we may never know. Several days later, military police shot and killed John Kalafatis as he sat in a car in Gaborone with several of his associates.

It was at first reported that the break-in had been at President Khama's sister's house, but it later emerged that it occurred at the home of a friend of the Khama family. What was stolen, and in fact all the details of the original burglary, were withheld from the media by both victim and police. The Kalafatis family hired a prominent human rights lawyer and succeeded in having John's body released for a private autopsy. He had been shot fifteen times at close range.

The officers of the military police who had shot John were tried for murder and sentenced to eleven years in jail. Before they had served a full year of that sentence, however, the President pardoned them and restored their military ranks. (In Canada, policemen who shoot suspects are hardly ever convicted.)

In 2012 unknown assailants shot John's father as he worked late in his workshop. He died several months later, it is said as the result of his injuries. In 2013 someone shot John's brother. He survived.

In February 2014, Dick Bayford, the above-mentioned Kalafatis family lawyer, told the press that the original burglary included the theft of a laptop on which there was a video of a homosexual orgy that involved a prominent state personality. (Gentle reader, you may remember that in the chapter about gender relations I told you that the President is widely assumed to be homosexual.) The wish to kill anyone who knew about the existence of such a video could explain the subsequent attempts to kill John's father and brother. But the bare facts are that no one involved admits to ever having seen or handled the laptop in question.

This story has been widely covered in the Botswana and even the Zimbabwe press. And there are some truly sensational blogs about it on the internet, such as the accusation that a British-Canadian secret agent was involved in the affair and that the police hate "coloureds", that is persons, such as the Kalafatis family, who are of mixed race. All this is pure sensationalism with not a shred of evidence to back it up. To return to reality, Wikileaks has published a cable that the American embassy wrote about the initial murder of John Kalafatis. But there are still many gaps in the story. What was the time lag between the initial burglary and the murder? Was the burglary ever solved? There must be a police report about that burglary. What about the transcripts of the trial of the military policemen? It was only spottily covered in the local press. And why was it the military police rather than the regular police who investigated a run-of-the-mill break-and-enter?

If any of you feel you would like a trip to Botswana and want to write a crime thriller, here is a story you can investigate, beginning with the material, such as the police report and trial transcripts that must be publicly available. And surely Bayford would be helpful. Take it away! It's up to you.

CHAPTER 7   ALL AROUND BOTSWANA

When I first came to Botswana, I approached it as a tourist rather than a resident or a worker. That first Christmas of 2008, various friends and family came to see me and the country. My husband Parkash and my son Paul were the first to arrive.

They were soon followed by a friend from Sudbury days, Shanta, who had recently and tragically lost her husband in a boating accident and who soon thereafter discovered a passion for travel. I was still in the guest house, and we soon filled it up, as there were just four rooms with private facilities. My dear friend Grace, whom I have known for over fifty years, arrived about two weeks later. And then, after Shanta and Grace had left, Paul's then-wife Raman arrived for a ten-day visit.

If the truth be told, Botswana is not much of a traditional tourist destination. Yes, I know the King of Spain went there to hunt elephants, but then would the King of Spain go to an ordinary place? Safaris and game watching, that is about it, and on safaris you can be lucky and see herds of elephants and prides of lions, or you might not see many animals at all. There is no way of making the animals appear when tourists want to see them, though I have been told that it is somewhat easier in the dry season — the Botswana winter between May and August — when the animals tend to cluster around their watering holes. But in December we were in the rainy season.

Background note: Botswana is a semi-arid country and the rainy season does not mean that it rains frequently or even once or twice a week. It rains from time to time, whereas during the dry winter period it does not rain at all. Guaranteed.

I had heard that there was malaria in the far north of Botswana, the Chobe, where many tourists go for game watching. And at that time the economic crisis in neighbouring Zimbabwe was at its worst. There was a breakdown of Zimbabwe's once-excellent infra-structure, and cholera spread across the border into Botswana, along the rivers that the two countries share. To me, inexperienced as I was, that sounded scary, and so I decided that we should do our safari in the northwestern part of Botswana, near the city of Maun (pronounced 'Mah-oon').

And since the cost of three motel rooms was expensive — even if Binnis was very reasonably priced and the University was paying for the room that Parkash and I occupied — I decided that we should go on safari as soon as possible. By the time we returned, my house would be ready.

Among the various drivers who looked for business around the Riverwalk mall and who used to drive me home after supper, I chose Syntax as the one most likely to be a good driver for the trip. His car, however, was not in the best condition, and it had no air conditioning. So we decided to rent a car from Avis Botswana. (I did not know then that we could have saved money by renting a car in South Africa and driving it across the border.) And since almost all cars in Botswana had manual transmissions at that time, only Syntax would be able to drive. All of us had driver's licences, but only Parkash had ever driven a car with a manual transmission, and that had been a long time ago. And besides, we were all used to driving on the right.

Syntax and I trekked out to the airport to rent a car. Back in 2008, that was the only place. We rented an air-conditioned car, and the next morning the five of us — Parkash, Paul, Shanta, Syntax and I — set out on our adventure. Except that when it comes to my family, early departures are a pipe dream. And Shanta and Syntax were no help in that department. Shanta said that she needed some money from the ATM; indeed I also needed extra cash. Syntax showed up good and early but without his luggage. So I had to accompany him to his place to pick up his stuff, then back to Binnis to pick up Shanta, and finally to the mall. There was a long line-up at the bank, and I wanted more money than the ATM would give me. I asked Syntax to stand in line for me while I found the foreign-linked ATMs for Shanta. When I came back — no sign of Syntax. He had decided that he absolutely had to buy a certain CD, and he had found someone else to stand in line for him! We finally connected and went back to Binnis to pick up Parkash and Paul, who fortunately were ready by then. It was already 11:00 am.

Our plan for the day was to make it to the town of Ghanzi, a centre of Basarwa culture. It proved to be a challenge, but we made it!

Not long after our 11:00 departure, some of us got hungry for lunch. Since supermarkets in Botswana sell hot food, we stopped at one in a small town. Fortunately no one needed to use a washroom because supermarkets do not come equipped. Next Syntax lost the road, and we found ourselves in front of the locked gate of a restricted-access diamond mine. (We did not have a motorist's map of Botswana. None seemed to be available in Gaborone. We had to rely on Syntax's expertise.)

We found the right road, and in the middle of the afternoon stopped at a nice guest house with a tearoom where we had tea and were able to use the facilities. There was a gas station nearby, but we still had quite a lot of gas. So we thought that we could wait to tank up. But by the time we were back on the road the gas started to disappear at an alarming rate, and there were no more gas stations. The needle soon was on empty. Syntax knew, as did I, that we would burn less gas if we drove fairly slowly. We did, and it started to get dark. Before we left Gaborone, Syntax and I had agreed that we would not travel at night, but what choice did we have?

In the dusk, a Botswana government transport truck signalled us to pull over. He only wanted to help us, to know why we were driving so slowly. We explained our dilemma, and he agreed to let us follow him, so that if we did run out of gas, he could help us. Fortunately, we were able to limp into a Shell station on the outskirts of Ghanzi before we ran out of gas. And the Shell station not only sold gas, it sold a road map of Botswana, which I have to this day.

We headed to the only hotel in town, the pleasant Ghanzi Arms. The hotel consisted of a central building with a restaurant and lobby and a number of round cabins built in the style of the traditional local houses, the rondavels, made of mud walls with a thatched roof. The hotel rondavels had concrete walls, but they did have thatched roofs, and each was equipped like a hotel room.

I had decided before the trip that we would stay in two rooms, Parkash, Paul and Syntax in one, Shanta and I in the other. Shanta was surprised that the hotels did not have communal sleeping facilities for drivers, as they do in India. I explained to her that Botswana was too egalitarian for that sort of thing. Perhaps, but I had not figured out Syntax. He did not say anything, but obviously he did not intend to spend the night in the same room with a couple of white foreigners. At every hotel we went to, he managed to persuade the staff to find him another place to sleep. It was all right with me as long as I did not have to pay for it. And as Syntax had brought little or no money with him, he was not paying either.

In the morning we went into town to find aspects of Basarwa culture. We were sent to a workshop where women accompanied by small children were making jewellery by hand. I found this scene rather depressing. The women were sitting on the ground in a dark space between two buildings, and children were playing in the dirt. We also visited two gift stores that sold Basarwa handicrafts.

But Syntax had been gathering his own information. "Don't you want to see a Basarwa village?" he asked. Well, yes, of course we did. So he took a detour off the main road until we came to a truly miserable place, a small community where the houses were made of cardboard and rags, and the children outside looked as if they were in urgent need of food. We tried giving them some coins, but they did not know what money was and did not take them. At the end of the row of miserable dwellings — I would not call them houses — stood a slightly more solid structure with a satellite TV reception dish on top. This, Syntax informed us, was the chief's house.

Basarwa women making jewellery to sell

At the Tropic of Capricorn with Paul and Parkash

Background note 1 — There are poor people in Gaborone, but the poverty in Botswana is much greater in the villages than in the towns and cities. In Gaborone there are a couple of poor neighbourhoods, the best-known of which is called Old Naledi, right in the city on the way to a large mall full of elegant shops. The houses in Old Naledi are mostly made of brick and concrete (as against metal sheets and wood and canvas scraps as in the South African townships), but there is no water supply to the individual houses. Instead there are "standpipes", communal water taps on the street corners, a system the government wants to get rid of because it allows people to waste water. Instead of a sewage system, there are outhouses behind the houses. These outhouses, as in most of the villages I visited, were made to a government-decreed design. They are built of stone or concrete, and there is a wall about three feet high around the front.

Locals like to tell stories of foreigners who land in Gaborone and ask a cab driver to take them to the poorest part of the city, which almost always brings them to Old Naledi with its cement houses. Local legend has it that such foreigners, especially if they have seen other African cities, often doubt that they have been shown the poverty they are seeking.

Background Note 2 — The Basarwa, or San, once called Bushmen, are the native people of Botswana, the ones who lived here before blacks settled in this dry country. They were a nomadic people who supported themselves by hunting game. South of Gaborone there are some ancient rock paintings, made by the ancestors of the Basarwa more than a thousand years ago. Some have faded, but some, such as a painting of giraffe and a zebra, are still clearly visible. The guide told us that the Basarwa would make pictures of the animals after they had eaten them, as a way of replacing what they had taken. One of the paintings, still quite clearly visible, is of a naked man.

The government of Botswana has made some efforts to integrate the Basarwa into the contemporary economy by giving them goats and farming implements and putting their children into boarding schools. This has not worked any more than it did in Canada. I remember a news report of a tragic incident where a young girl of eight had gone home for the weekend. When her older brother walked her back to the boarding school on Sunday evening, she pretended to go into the school but instead tried to walk back home through the bush. She was killed by wild animals. And yet one of my colleagues, a woman with a British PhD, said to me, "What are they complaining about? We have to pay to send our children to boarding school."

Botswana's wealth is built on high-quality diamonds, and the government moved some Basarwa from their traditional hunting grounds to get access to a particularly valuable diamond deposit. This caused a British-based NGO, Survival International, to accuse the government of selling "blood diamonds", like those that helped to spark the extraordinarily violent and cruelty-filled civil war in Sierra Leone. Survival International called for a boycott of Botswana diamonds. The Botswana government hired an American public relations firm to tell the world their side of the story. It worked; Botswana is still selling diamonds.

I am with the government of Botswana on this one. The government has used the country's diamond wealth to give Batswana a better life: clean drinking water, universal free primary education and government-paid medical care. The Basarwa have not always been treated well, and like the native people in Canada, they have insisted on their rights to hunt, instead of taking up farming. And there is widespread and deep seated prejudice against them. When I mentioned to one of the young professors that there might be some Basarwa women among the cleaning staff at the University, he was incredulous. The University would never hire one of them! The grandfather of the current president of the country had several wives, one of whom was a Mosarwa. She was not the grandmother of the president, however, who is descended from the last and youngest of the old chief's wives, a cousin and thus of suitable royal blood.

> One of the best of Botswana's many newspapers is Mmegi, and this paper commissioned a historical study that gives the best and most thorough account of the life of the President's grandfather and his various wives. Interestingly, the Mmegi account concludes with the statement that "the insinuation that she [the President's grandmother] was a Mosarwa" is due to the fact that one of the wives did in fact belong to that group. The use of the pejorative term "insinuation" is surely significant.
>
> As for a Mosarwa member of parliament, that is as yet only a remote possibility.

We then took the road north to Maun, which was paved and marked with a central line. Soon we had to cross the "veterinary fence". This is a government measure to stop diseases spreading from wild animals to the domestic kind and vice versa. Of course, the government cannot build enough fences to stop wild animals from going wherever they want, but farmers are responsible for making sure that their livestock does not cross this barrier. On the road, each car has to stop and be inspected, and the passengers have to walk through a footbath that disinfects their shoes.

There was yet another police barrier on the road. This one checked cars for illegal immigrants from Zimbabwe. As we were heading north, that did not make too much sense to me. But who knows....

The road to Maun was picturesque. We saw farmers with donkey carts as well as ostriches strolling through the underbrush.

When we reached Maun, we had trouble finding a place to stay. The places recommended by the *Lonely Planet* guide were all unsuitable, far out of town or impossible to find. We tried a place with Greek owners, but that one, motel-like, did not have air conditioning in all the units and looked grim and not too clean. We finally headed to the most expensive hotel in town, when right across the road we saw a new and attractive medium-size hotel called The Rhino Lodge. It had two rooms left, a small single room for Syntax and a large family room which the rest of us could share. I have a lovely picture of Shanta crouching on the floor, Indian-style, making tea for all of us.

The owner was more than willing to help us arrange a safari. And the girl on the front desk, who had been to tourism school, had done her internship at Disneyworld in Florida. We felt well looked after.

The owner ran the possibilities for a safari trip by us. We could set out with an all-equipped tent, meals would be prepared for us, and we could do "game drives" to see animals. None of us was a camper, but we agreed because that seemed to be the thing to do. About half an hour later, someone appeared at our room to enquire about dietary restrictions. After we had settled the breakfast menu, I asked about tea and coffee. The guy gave me a strange look.

A little later, the owner appeared at our door. He said that he had decided that camping might not be suitable for us. There was a camp with cottages from which we would be able to do our game watching. We agreed enthusiastically.

The next morning, Mark, our guide, arrived in a jeep to pick up the four of us and take us game watching. There was a wedding planned for the hotel that evening, and the management was happy that we were vacating our room. We vacated the big room and left Syntax and the rented car behind. We piled most of our luggage into Syntax's room and just took a little overnight bag each. Syntax was happy because he had an old school friend in Maun who worked in an electronics store. They borrowed a machine and DVDs and spent the evening watching films. Dear Syntax had not brought any money with him; I gave him an advance on his wages so that he could buy food.

After he picked us up, Mark the driver of the jeep and our nature guide for the trip made several stops in the town before we hit the road. Finally, after 11:00 am — the Mahant family starting time — we were on the road and off to see animals. There was nothing much at first, only a couple of ostriches. Then we stopped for a picnic lunch. One of our stops had been to pick up a cooler full of food, including sandwiches, fruit, cookies and cold drinks. Did I mention how fond Batswana are of cookies?

Mark was an excellent guide. There is a special course at a college in Maun where the drivers and nature guides train. It is a course of only six months, but it produces amazing results. Mark could spot animals at a great distance and tell us how old they were, whether they were pregnant, whether they were part of a herd (even if there was no herd in sight). I found the same in 2014 when I went on a "game drive" with friends. The guides were amazing.

After lunch, we started to see animals. There were a number of giraffes chewing on the leaves of the tree they prefer. The giraffes looked majestic and were not afraid of visitors. They stared at us with a look which said, "What are you doing in our territory?" We took a picture of Parkash standing right next to one of the animals who did not even deign to turn away.

There were zebras and monkeys and more ostriches, but only one lone elephant. Mark said it was probably an old one that had been expelled from its herd. Shanta was disappointed. She had hoped to see a whole herd of elephants.

By four o'clock or so we arrived at our camp. There were cabins in the shape of rondavels, just as there had been in Ghanzi. Each room was equipped with two beds covered with mosquito nets, a bathroom and a carafe of drinking water. This remote area did not have access to electricity lines, but there was a diesel-powered generator that supplied the rondavels with electricity from 5:00 to 10:00 pm. Except that none of us goes to bed by ten, so the staff kindly left the generator on a bit longer.

After we had deposited our luggage, Mark took us for another game drive. We went to a river, or perhaps it was a lake, where a large herd of hippos was bathing and playing. We took many pictures, and there were other jeeps full of tourists doing the same. Then it started to rain, and it was also getting dark. So we turned back. The rain intensified. The jeep was covered with an awning, but this rain seemed to be driving in from the sides. There was no escaping it. Paul sat in the front, next to Mark, and he got soaked first. Parkash and I were in the backseat and Shanta in the far back. I don't mind getting wet — I am after all from Vancouver — but I need to protect my glasses so that I can see. I tried to curl up in a fetal position, burying my head in Parkash's shoulder. This way I thought that my back might get wet, but my face would be spared, but it was of no use. All of us were soaked to the skin. Mark, amazingly, kept right on driving on the unpaved road in the dark as though nothing was happening.

After we regained our cabins, we tried to dry off as best we could using towels and my hair dryer. Since we were intending only to stay overnight, we had not even brought a complete change of clothing. Then we took our still slightly moist selves to the dining hall for dinner. We were the only guests that night. The two ladies who ran the place had prepared a tasty dinner. Before each course, one of them stood in the corner and announced what we would be eating.

These two ladies had also been to tourism school and were making good use of their skills. I learned later that this tourist facility was run by the Basarwa. They had been given a land grant by the government and had then negotiated an agreement whereby they could lease out part of the land and use the proceeds to start this tourist camp and train themselves to run it.

The next morning, after we enjoyed a tasty breakfast, Mark came by to take us on one more game drive, this time into the Moremi Game Reserve. Unfortunately we did not see many interesting animals there. I remember a herd of water antelopes and an ostrich with a broken wing. Mark said that a lion may have tried to tear it off, but there was no sign of lions.

Then it was time to head back to Maun. We stopped by the road for yet another packed lunch which Mark once again provided. This time there were lots of cookies. We ate as much as we wanted, then we gave the rest to a circle of little boys who had appeared out of nowhere and had been watching us eat. They were delighted with their treats, picking out the pink wafer cookies and eating them first.

Back in Maun, we reunited with Syntax and once again took possession of our hotel room, which the wedding guests had by then vacated. The next morning we began our return journey to Gaborone. This time we took another road, one that curved through the eastern part of the country. This road took us to Serowe, the capital of the Bangwato tribe and the home of Botswana's first and fourth presidents, Seretse Khama and his son Ian Khama.

We had not seen much game. I thought that perhaps it was my mistake to have gone to Maun instead of Kasane in the far north of Botswana. In February 2014 a group of friends and I did go to Kasane. We stayed in a nice hotel, the Chobe Safari Lodge, and took a couple of game drives as well as two boat rides on the river to observe animals there. This time we did see a herd of elephants as well as some crocodiles, even a few wild dogs, which are hard to find — but no lions, cheetahs or rhinos. I guess what you see is partly a matter of luck.

The eastern route from Maun to Serowe was not as well paved or well supplied with services as the road to Ghanzi had been. For lunch we visited a primitive village restaurant where I could not understand several of the terms on the menu and had to ask Syntax to translate. There were chickens running around underfoot, even in the eating area, and the sanitary facilities consisted of outhouses.

I had hoped that we would be able to spend the night in the Khama Rhino Sanctuary, which is about 20 km north of Serowe. This is a wildlife preserve especially for rhinos, where they are protected from their only predators — humans — who steal their horns and sell them in Asia for their supposed aphrodisiac qualities. The sanctuary includes a number of cottages where visitors can stay overnight, so that they can see the rhinos first thing in the morning or at dusk in the evening. Unfortunately all the cabins were booked. I did not manage to visit the Sanctuary until 2012, when Parkash and I attended a wedding in Serowe and we went there afterwards. Then we did see many rhinos as well as birds in an aviary and other wildlife including jackals. Apparently the local farmers are not too keen on having the Sanctuary nearby, because the jackals and other predators cannot be harmed, and the animals are smart enough to know that they can help themselves to a farmer's chickens and then return to the Sanctuary.

On that December evening in 2008, however, we had to continue on to Serowe. Syntax suggested that we stay in the Serowe Hotel, and I should have listened to him. The guidebook said that there was another hotel on a prominent ridge that had character and was architecturally interesting, consisting of cabins built into a hillside. So we went there. The hotel had vacancies and offered to make us supper. The food was pretty awful — tough beef, frozen vegetables — but the rooms looked all right at first glance. Syntax, as usual, made his own arrangements, while Parkash and Paul took a cabin near the dining area, not too far up the hill. Shanta and I got a cabin further up the hillside.

When we got to our room, we found that the shower was defective, though it produced some water, and the TV did not work. When we opened up the bed, the sheets were covered with thousands of little bugs. There was no way we were going back down that hill to ask for another room. It was dark, and the stone staircase looked none too safe. I have a balancing problem intensified by a lazy eye that makes it difficult for me to go down any stairs, let alone unfamiliar steps, without a railing in the dark. We used the flat side of the useless television remote to brush the bugs off the sheets and slept as best we could.

Next morning, the breakfast was quite decent. We learned that Paul and Parkash had changed rooms when their television also did not work. Fortunately, they did not encounter bugs.

Wishing the hotel a not-so-fond farewell, we explored the pleasant little town and visited the Khama family museum. The Khamas had been a leading family and the chiefs of the Bangwato tribe when missionaries first came to the Bechuanaland Protectorate in the nineteenth century. In 1966, when Botswana became an independent country, it was Seretse Khama who became its first president. Not that the British colonial authorities made his path an easy one. He had studied in England and married an Englishwoman. When he wanted to return to Bechuanaland, hoping to take up the chieftainship of his tribe, the British at first tried to hold up his return, and when that proved impossible, prevented him from taking over as chief, in spite of the clearly expressed wishes of the members of the tribe. The reason was not that he headed up an independence movement — by this time the British were trying to rid themselves of colonies — but the fact that white South Africans, with their strict apartheid rules next door, would not tolerate such a marriage on their doorstep. Just across the border, a paramount chief with a white wife? In the apartheid worldview, not now, not ever.

> *Historical background note: The British had their scruples about their racist policy. In 1949 they commissioned an inquiry into the question as to who should be the chief of the Bangwato. The resulting (1951) report was suppressed and only released in recent years at the request of historians. The report argues that at a time when Namibia was still ruled by South Africa and Southern Rhodesia was also ruled by a racist regime, Bechuanaland, as it was then called, was completely surrounded by apartheid regimes (except for the river crossing at the Zambian border, which the report does not mention). As a landlocked country, the British argued, Bechuanaland could not afford to offend its neighbours on whom it was dependent for the transit of all its imports and exports.*

A summary of this story, along with various family keepsakes and items of furniture, are on display in the Khama house, now a museum. Unfortunately we were never able to revisit the Khama house, even on one occasion when I phoned ahead to ask to see it. It seemed to be open only a few hours on weekdays and not on weekends.

One room in the Khama house was devoted to the memory of Bessie Head, who is considered to be the country's national writer, though I prefer the novels by Unity Dow, who is our contemporary. Bessie Head lived from 1937–1986, and her novel *When Rain Clouds Gather* is often required reading in the country's secondary schools. A retired English professor from UB leads a group that is now working to create a separate memorial site for Bessie, a task that will be easier now that Bessie's only child, a son, has died intestate, and more of her papers and possessions will become available. The memorial will be housed in the home that she and her son occupied in Serowe.

Bessie Head was a refugee from apartheid South Africa. Her mother was white, and there are various versions of the story of her birth. Wikipedia says that her mother had a relationship with a black servant. Since interracial sex was illegal in South Africa, the mother was declared insane and sent to an asylum, where she was safe from being punished for the crime of miscegenation. One of the people working on the biography and the memorial told me that the mother *was* mentally ill and that she returned to the asylum from a visit home, pregnant. The child was given to a white family to adopt, but when infant Bessie turned out to be black, she was taken away and given to a coloured family. As an adult, Bessie Head was unwilling to throw any light on the story, if she even knew it. She, after all, had not been born when many of the key events happened.

Bessie Head's principal language was English. She spoke Zulu, Afrikaans and Setswana only imperfectly. Yet she is considered an icon of Botswana literature and was awarded Botswana citizenship on that basis, without the usual formalities.

Bessie first became a primary school teacher in Serowe after she settled in Botswana, later a full-time writer. Heavy drinking contributed to her death in 1986. Her son Howard suffered from a mild case of fetal alcohol syndrome. A friend of mine attended the same boarding school as the boy, adjoining Bessie's yard in Serowe, and she says that the adolescent was known to run through the girls' dorms — naked. Howard died in 2010 of septicaemia brought on by HIV/AIDS and a huge Christmas binge on whiskey.

Before we leave the subject of Botswana literature, Unity Dow's *The Screaming of the Innocent* is one of the best thrillers I have ever read. That does not say much because I do not read many thrillers, but people do agree with me that it is an excellent example of its genre, and besides it gives an insight into contemporary Botswana life. It is a good read whether or not you ever plan to visit Botswana.

And now back to Serowe in December 2008. We — Syntax, Parkash, Paul, Shanta and I — drove back to Gaborone, a trip of less than four hours. On the way, Syntax had one more tourist sight to show us. He stopped at a large sign indicating that we were crossing the Tropic of Capricorn. We took pictures draped over the sign. We were really far south!

The day after we returned to Gaborone, we moved into my university house. It was also the day my friend Grace arrived from Canada. Because she was disappointed that we had already done a safari and a tour around Botswana, I tried hard to find other touristy things to do in and around Gaborone.

About thirty kilometres south of Gaborone, near the village of Kanye, there is a tree under which David Livingstone is supposed to have preached a century and a half ago. It is a big, bushy tree now. Nearby there are some ancient rock paintings, and in 2008 they were behind a tall wire fence. The man who controlled the gate was not there on Thursdays, and it happened to be a Thursday. We could just see a faint outline of the paintings in the distance. (When I returned in 2015, the rock paintings were open to visitors seven days a week.) Grace was not having good luck with her sightseeing. On another day, we went downtown and visited the National Museum, which is really more for schoolchildren than for tourists. On that day, we also tried to see the Anglican cathedral, but it was closed until after New Year's (still more than a week away).

My Belfast friends at the guest house really liked a tourist camp just south of Gaborone, called Mokolodi after a nearby village. This camp is operated by an environmental NGO which uses the proceeds to run environmental education programs in elementary schools.

The Mokolodi camp consists of a number of tourist cottages built around a watering hole for wild animals. The cottages have one to three bedrooms and include a well-equipped kitchen and a barbecue. The idea is that you bring your own food and prepare it in the kitchen and/or on the barbecue. Then you can sit at the dining table on the patio and watch the animals come to the watering hole. Shanta, who is a vegetarian, took charge of the food and made us an excellent Indian meal. (In preparation, we had visited Gaborone's vegetarian supermarket, Mr. Veg.) We did not see many animals in the evening, mostly a few warthogs, but in the morning there were more, including a giraffe which had to kneel to drink from the watering hole. None of us had ever seen a kneeling giraffe.

In addition to the basic stay at a cottage, Mokolodi sells side trips. The cottage stays are reasonably priced, especially on a weekday. The extras tend to be pricey. Nevertheless, I bought an up-close-and-personal session with the cheetahs for Paul and me. Paul was afraid to pet the cheetahs, but did so — very gently.

In the jeep, on the way to the cheetah place, I overheard on the internal communication system that the people who had bought the visits with the rhinos were not seeing any rhinos that morning (though my Belfast friends did when they went). If you really want to see rhinos, I recommend that you go the Khama Rhino Sanctuary, as described above.

Mokolodi is great if you like to get away from it all — no television, no cell phone coverage, and lights that are so dim it is difficult to read. For me, one night of getting away from it all was definitely enough.

One of the most interesting sights in Gaborone is the monument to The Three Chiefs, who travelled to England in 1895 to plead with the colonial government not to hand Bechuanaland over to Cecil Rhodes's private company. They succeeded, and as Neil Parsons points out in his book *King Khama, Emperor Joe and the Great White Queen* (University of Chicago Press, 1998) this outcome was as much due to Cecil Rhodes's failure as it was to their success. Rhodes infuriated the Colonial Secretary by attempting to take control of the Boer republics in South Africa with his own private army, an attack that failed miserably. After that, Rhodes was not likely to get anything from the British government.

Yet the three chiefs are rightly revered as the founders of the Tswana nation. Their propaganda campaign was brilliant. The Colonial Secretary was Joseph Chamberlain, whose political base lay in the Birmingham area with its Methodist population. The three chiefs travelled throughout England, accompanied by their missionary friend and interpreter, William Willoughby, and accused Rhodes of wanting to introduce alcoholic beverages into the Bechuanaland territory. The Methodists were asked to write letters to the government, particularly the Colonial Secretary, to stop Rhodes from taking over. It reminds me of Amnesty International, which after all was founded in England in the 1970s.

The monument in Gaborone consists of a large open concrete court, with oversized statues of the three chiefs at one end and historical inscriptions in Setswana on plinths along the sides. During normal working hours there is a guide to tell the story. Not the most beautiful of monuments, but one that is worth seeing, and one that is ignored by the tourist books. The monument demonstrates that the Batswana enjoyed a common identity as early as the mid-1800s, which may in part account for the relative success of their economy and political system today.

Another touristy activity near Gaborone are the potteries, which I have already described in Chapter 2. The drive out to the villages where the potteries are located is a pleasant one, through countryside that is somewhat greener than Gaborone itself. Unfortunately, the road back into the city passes through a suburb filled with many hectares of used car lots.

There is also a game reserve in Gaborone itself. I have not visited it, but my son Paul and his ex-wife Raman did, with Syntax doing the driving. Syntax reported that the road was unpaved and covered his car with mud, and that there were not many animals to be seen.

Even if Gaborone and its suburbs hold one-quarter of Botswana's population, Botswana is still a country of villages. The nightly news is mostly about villages, and nearly everyone comes from a village, even if s/he lives in a city. The problem for an expatriate like me is that it is easy to get to know the friendly people of the city, but to get to know a village is quite different. I had seen a bit of some villages when attending weddings and funerals and in my search for a real African church, but that is not the same as learning about village life.

So when my husband and I were coming back from a wedding in Serowe, I asked Syntax to take us to his village. This village is a large one, with a police station, a school, two soccer fields, a little store, a clinic, the village council and even a guest house. Syntax took us to see his family's yard, where the main family house stands and where his elder sister and a brother (both unmarried) live. (Syntax has many siblings because his mother died when he was little; his father then married a woman who already had children, and after that the two of them had more children together.

Next door was the small concrete house that Syntax has built for himself. Both houses are made of concrete blocks, and Syntax's has running water. But neither he nor his sister has electricity in the house. Sarah's family does not have electricity either. There is a sizeable fee for the connection, and the electricity itself is expensive. So most villagers forego that luxury, which means that they also must make do without refrigerators or fans. But somehow everyone manages to find a place to charge a cell phone.

Syntax's family does not have any livestock, only a few chickens. His brother and sister farm a piece of land on which they grow corn and sorghum and a few watermelons. They have none of the cash income which would come with livestock. They walk to the fields every day and walk back in the evening. Any money they have comes from the brothers who live in the city. I have read about subsistence farming; here I was seeing it for real. The sister seemed all right with the situation, but the brother had a hopeless look in his eye that haunted me for weeks.

Syntax explained that the government assigned a tractor or two to every village and that the families in the village could book the use of the tractor during the officially designated ploughing season. Some farmers use donkeys for transport and farm work. We did not see any donkeys in Syntax's village, though in the north we did see farmers with donkey carts.

Syntax told us that Sarah's family was better off than his. They had some goats. But he said that we could not visit Sarah's family — where his older son was staying with Sarah's mother — because in order to go to her house he had to dress up in a shirt and jacket, and he had not brought such clothes with him on the driving trip. I found all of that strange because shirts and jackets were hardly traditional Tswana attire. Before the Europeans came to sub-Saharan Africa, animal skins were the usual form of clothing. That is why, when the Three Chiefs paid a courtesy call to Queen Victoria, they gave her a ceremonial outfit of animal skins. The Three Chiefs, by the way, wore suits when they addressed Methodist congregations and when they visited Queen Victoria. Where did this idea about suits come from? And about Syntax not being allowed to visit his son? There are some questions that even my best local friends would or could not answer.

Syntax explained that the local police dealt with various minor crimes, and that the clinic was staffed by a nurse and a doctor who visited from time to time. I asked whether the police would deal with cases of spousal abuse or the neglect of children. He said that a social worker visited the clinic once a week to deal with such cases.

The most pleasant part of the visit to the village was Syntax's auntie's yard. The auntie supported herself by looking after the children of relatives who worked in the city. There were six I think, which must have given the auntie a comfortable income. We were there in the afternoon, just after the older children had come home from school. They all sat on a blanket so that we could photograph them, and they were happy to receive the small boxes of cookies that I passed out.

One aspect of village life that I longed to see was a *moraka* or cattlepost. Any family of any substance has, in addition to a farm, a moraka where a *modisa* or herdsman carries out the daily chores. (The word refers to anyone who looks after animals, as in the 23rd Psalm.) Villagers grow crops within walking distance of their village homes, but beef cattle require more space. So many families own another piece of land, within driving distance of the village, where the cattle are kept. If well-managed, most cows give birth every year. Thus any successful farmer soon has an ever-growing herd. (When I returned to Botswana in 2015, I learned that some farmers who kept purebred herds had begun to use artificial insemination.)

Cattle posts are by their nature remote, but I was determined to see one. Finally my colleague Dorothy agreed to take me to the cattlepost she and her husband had recently acquired (though they are city dwellers). Her son drove us over some dirt roads in a four-wheel-drive vehicle, and when we reached the cattlepost we ate the sandwich lunch she had packed. Their employee, the modisa, lived in a little hut, so small that he kept his crockery and cooking pot outside on a shelf.

As it was the end of the month, Dorothy delivered groceries for the month as well as the modisa's pay and Christmas presents for his children. His wife and children lived in a village about 5 km away so that the children could go to school. The reason that not all of Botswana's children go to school is that people take them to the cattle posts where there are no schools. This modisa's children were not living in the bush, but the children of a modisa from a nearby moraka were hanging around — our visit was a major event — and presumably they did not go to school.

I had visited a moraka, but really there was not much to see. Some cows and chickens were running around. That was about it.

There is a sequel to this story. A couple of months later Dorothy informed me that the herdsman's wife with their five children had moved in with another man. She thought it was funny, but it must have been sad for the modisa. For Dorothy, it meant fewer presents to bring, as the children now belonged to another family. But when I returned in 2015 this herdsman had acquired a new partner with three children of her own.

> *Background note: In Botswana, women almost always get to keep the children when a couple separates, especially if the couple, as is often the case, is not married. A friend of mine divorced her husband when the children were teenagers, and she ended up paying for*

their education, which included foreign universities for both of them. In some cases, when an unmarried couple has children and are separated, the father is expected (and can be ordered by a court) to pay support, especially when the mother does not have enough income to support the child or children. I heard of one case, where the mother was a professor at UB and the father a businessman, where the custody of the children (still in primary school) was awarded to the father — but the children lived with the mother and spent time with their father during the holidays.

Dorothy told me the story about the modisa in 2015, when she took me and my friend Rosemary to see her husband's latest venture, a goat farm on the outskirts of a village not far from Gaborone. The goat farm is outside the main village, and when we drove to and from the farm, the three of us squeezed into the front seat of a small truck. (The truck was a four-wheel-drive one with two gear shifts. I sat in the middle and could squeeze in by putting my feet on the dashboard.) On our return from the goat farm, we saw a middle-aged couple hitchhiking. Dorothy stopped and offered them the back of the truck, and later when another couple of people were hitchhiking, she picked them up too. We dropped all four of them in the village. I expressed some surprise that Dorothy would pick up people when her truck was already quite full, but she explained that she needed to do this if she recognized the people. Later, if she and her husband needed extra help, those people would be there for them. I have my doubts about the communal solidarity of traditional life, which often includes a fair dose of oppression and exploitation, especially of women and children. But there are times, such as this one, when it holds together and even has its charming aspects. It is this sense of solidarity that works for all — well, most — of Botswana.

CHAPTER 8   UNIVERSITY LIFE

Gentle readers, I have left this topic to the end, on the assumption that it would not interest all of you. The internal goings-on of a university are of little interest to those who live outside the ivory tower, and even they often have enough of this topic once they leave the hallowed walls. Some decades ago, a British novelist, C.P. Snow, wrote novels that were set in Oxford University and described the machinations of university politics there. The novels were successful enough to earn Snow a seat in the House of Lords, but they have been all but forgotten since. Robertson Davies's *Rebel Angels* is an equally forgotten Canadian novel, set in a Canadian university. You get the point; universities do not make suitable settings for good stories. Otherwise, university life — deservedly — plays only a cameo role in literature, as in Alexander McCall Smith's novel *The Tears of the Giraffe* (set in Botswana, of course), Margaret Laurence's The *Diviners,* or in an earlier age, Hugh McLennan's *The Watch that Ends the Night* and Thomas Hardy's *Jude the Obscure.* As for non-fiction, universities only appear in the news occasionally, usually when some-one complains of underfunding, boasts of some obscure research project or when there has been some scandal with sexual undertones.

So the internal life of universities deservedly does not attract much attention. This is as it should be. What happens at universities is not nearly as important as those who run the universities think it is. Thus the purpose of this introduction is to advise you, gentle readers, that you may want to skip this chapter and live happily in the belief that you have read the entire book and can add it to your Facebook list of books read.

When I first arrived in Gaborone, the department chair and the university housing manager met me at the airport. They drove me to the guest house (described in Chapter 1) and gave me time to rest, shower and change my clothes. The next morning after breakfast some-one arrived to walk me to the University.

My university life in Botswana began, as I guess it does anywhere in the world, with a large number of forms to fill out. The University of Botswana is not an easy place to navigate. All buildings are numbered, but the numbers appear to be in the order in which the buildings were occupied. Similar numbers are not necessarily in the same area. There are walking paths and driving roads, but I found it very difficult to find my way around, even after more than a year in the place. The department chair had wisely anticipated this problem. He provided me with a teaching assistant as a full-time guide for the first week. I immediately dubbed this man, a tall Kalanga, my guardian angel. He was most helpful, and he and I are still in touch on Facebook.

The formalities included applying for a work permit. This involved filling out many more forms, but I was relieved to learn that I did not have to stand in any lines at the Ministry of Labour, which in Botswana deals with immigration matters. The University has one employee, a woman, who is a specialist on immigration issues. She takes all the staff applications to the Ministry and has built up such a good knowledge of the process that nearly everyone who applies gets the necessary work permit (more on that later).

The formalities also included a medical exam, which consisted primarily of some blood tests and a chest X-ray. This was a university, not a government, requirement, which I found quite unnecessary since I was, because of my age, not eligible for the medical and life insurance coverage the University provides for its employees. (In Botswana basic health care is provided free by the government to all citizens, and the University provides additional coverage to its full-time employees). The Ugandan doctor who did the examination was so interested in chatting with me about Canada and African politics that the guardian angel and the department chair (who had driven me there) eventually sent the receptionist to ask why I was taking so long.

Other formalities included opening a bank account, as all employees are paid by direct deposit. The banks in Botswana (The major ones are South African and British-owned.) are modern and for the most part quite efficient, except for the long line-ups at the end of the month, since no one seems to have thought of staggering paydays. As described in the chapter on crime, I developed a good working relationship with my bank.

I was also pleased to note that the department provided me with an office from day 1 on the campus. Indeed an air-conditioned office was one of the conditions in my contract. I was fortunate, because some junior faculty had to share offices, or even share offices in another building, whereas my office was located in the main social science building, just around the corner from the secretary and the department chair. Within a couple of days, I was teaching, much to the relief of the professors who had been subbing for me.

Botswana's first president, Sir Seretse Khama, decided that the country needed its own university. At the time of independence, the country had been much neglected by the British, who considered it a worthless backwater. There were only a few secondary schools, only the most basic of medical facilities and not a single dentist. Before the wealth of the newly discovered diamonds started to flow into the economy, a university was a tremendous undertaking that the country could scarcely afford. Khama had a solution: He asked each farmer to donate one cow or bull. Cattle were, after all, the country's principal source of wealth. With the money raised from the sale of these animals, the government would found a university. That is why at the centre of the campus, in front of the library, there is a statue of a bull being herded to the kraal.

The University now enrols more than 15 000 students in many faculties, including engineering, medicine, law, agriculture and business. There are also some unusual specialties, such as archeology and archival studies in the faculty of humanities and population studies (demography) in the social sciences. Undergraduate courses are free for citizens of Botswana and for the children of the faculty and other employees. Graduate students have to pay fees, which are, however, often covered by their employers.

With students in the new classroom block at UB

A bull being herded to market — UB's original funding model

Undergraduate students who finished high school with good grades, roughly the equivalent of a B+, not only receive free undergraduate education, they are also paid a living allowance and given grants for the purchase of books, lab equipment and USB sticks — as well as two trips home per year if they do not live in Gaborone. Students with lower but passing grades can still attend UB, but they need to pay their own fees.

Most students do not work to supplement their income. I had students in my third- and fourth-year classes who had never worked a day in their lives. This was not universally true. Foreign students and unfunded students do work, sometimes as store clerks or taxi drivers. Some run small businesses on the side. One enterprising fellow set up a computer, printer, and small portable generator just outside the pedestrian gate into the campus. Students were thus able to print their assignments without having to leave campus. As I mentioned in Chapter 6, a graduate student I knew started a business selling advertising for flyers that were then inserted into newspapers, and he did quite well at that.

In early 2009 the government reduced the maintenance grants paid to students by about 30%. This resulted in large-scale strikes and demonstrations.

> *Some context: the maintenance allowance was reduced from about three times what a full-time maid earns in a month to about twice that amount.*

The students at first walked out with almost 100% observance of the strike. They also marched to the Ministry of Finance in the government district, where police action resulted in injuries to one student. The university administration retaliated by shutting down the University, but I did not receive the email that informed staff of this fact. Although I had had a UB email address since September, for some strange reason my address was not on the Vice-Chancellor's list of all staff. That should have been automatic. (The IT department at UB left much to be desired, though the situation improved somewhat over the years.)

That day, after the big student demonstration, I had been off-campus at lunchtime. When I came back, I encountered hundreds of students streaming out of the gate, many of them carrying or dragging suitcases. When I reached my office, there was no one around, no colleagues, no support staff. I could see no physical danger, no fire or fumes nor could I hear any emergency sirens or vehicles. I decided that this was an opportunity to get caught up on email. During the working day, the internet became very slow. Now with so many people gone, it would surely be working better. It did. I went to my office and spent two to three happy hours on the internet. Finally, I called someone to see what had happened. I learned that the University had been closed, so I set out for home.

But that turned out not to be so easy. I took the elevator down to the quad and started walking toward the pedestrian gate, where I could catch a combi home. But I did not get very far. A security guard accosted me and told me that the pedestrian gate was closed and that I could not walk that way. Only the main gate, near the administration building, was open. I played dumb and said that I did not know the way to that gate. So a security guard accompanied me. As we walked through the open square of what was then the student centre (UB has since built a big fancy new student centre.), I saw a strange sight. Twenty-four policemen and women, forming a rectangular formation, stood in the open square. A commander was putting them through their paces; it must have been something like turn left, stand at ease, that kind of stuff. The empty campus, the police — it all felt a bit creepy. But I reached the gate and later my home without trouble, though I had to walk quite a ways to get to my usual combi stop.

After that, I used the opportunity of the enforced holiday to make a quick trip to Cape Town.

A couple of weeks later classes resumed, though attendance was still below normal. One morning, the week after classes resumed, I was teaching a large undergraduate class on the ground floor of the social science building. Suddenly all the students got up and started running for the door. I had no idea what the problem was but decided that discretion was the better part of valour. I picked up my purse and lecture notes and followed the students into the quad outside. Students were also pouring out of the other classrooms. The crush of running students was so great that I was pushed against a wall. The bodies scrambling past me forced my purse and lecture materials out of my hands. Fortunately, one of my students saw what had happened and picked up my stuff for me.

In the distance, I could see what had caused the disturbance. Masked persons carrying long staves were approaching the building. These were the determined militants who wanted to continue the strike and were threatening to beat the students who had gone to class. I reported the incident to the dean. I do not know what steps the administration took to resolve the problem, but after that day, classes continued uninterrupted.

There were other strikes of undergraduate students during my time at UB. The undergraduate curriculum was rigid, as were the teaching methods. Much of what was taught consisted of rote learning followed by exams. No wonder the students became frustrated. Strikes of one type or another were an annual occurrence. (The graduate programs were of a higher quality, at least in political science.)

Another strike of some consequence occurred during my final year at UB. The drinking of alcohol was only allowed in a few designated areas of the campus: in a faculty lounge attached to one of the staff cafeterias and in an undergraduate pub located in a temporary building near the centre of the campus, not far from the graduate student apartments. That pub caused problems, because at night noisy under-graduates kept awake graduate students who said they needed to study.

In 2012, I think it was in February in the middle of term, the administration announced that they were closing the student pub, as the land would be needed for the construction of a new building. Naturally this resulted in a strike and demonstrations. Once again the administration closed the University.

In spite of its initial forceful reaction, the administration later backed down and allowed the pub to stay in business. I told anyone who would listen that it was stupid to try to close the pub in midterm. Someone must have heard me. During the long winter break, in July 2013, the pub disappeared. When the students arrived in August, it was gone.

> *The regulation of the consumption of alcohol is a controversial subject in Botswana. It is part of the country's political history. In 1895, when the three chiefs persuaded the Colonial Secretary not to give the Bechuanaland territory to Cecil Rhodes's private company, one of their principal arguments was that Rhodes would allow the sale of alcohol. Rumour has it that Botswana's first president, Sir Seretse Khama, was an alcoholic, and that is why his son, the current president, Ian Khama, is so determined to toughen the alcohol laws. There has been surprisingly little discussion of raising the legal drinking age, which is a liberal 18 years.*

As for the students, there are a number of restaurants with liquor licenses and at least one sleazy pub within a 20- to 30-minute walk from the campus, so that closing the on-campus pub did not deprive the students of alcohol. Whether forcing students to do their drinking off-campus is a good idea is another question.

I should add that graduate students did not usually participate in the strikes. They paid for their courses. It was only during the first strike noted above, when the campus was not considered safe, that they did not come to class.

Undergraduate students all over the world are ingenious when it comes to dreaming up excuses for late work, and any professor worth his or her chalk should be able to compile an amusing essay of such stories. I remember a conference in Denmark where a Dutch professor told me that the death rate among his students' grandmothers had decreased greatly since he started to require a proof of death, such as a newspaper obituary.

Here are two Botswana examples of excuses with local cultural flavour. One was a student who presented me and another professor with a long, turgid letter, stating that he had had unprotected sex after drinking and that he was so afraid of having contracted HIV that he could not concentrate on his work. He besought us to keep this information confidential because his mother worked on campus, and he did not want her to find out about his problem. Both of us gave this excuse the response it deserved.

Another student came from a farming family in the central town of Serowe. He told me that he had not been able to complete his essay because he had had to rush home to look after the cattle — because the family modisa had been struck by lightning. I gave him the benefit of the doubt (though I doubted his story) because he was an otherwise serious student who showed an interest in his work, and also perhaps because of the ingenuity of his story.

The administration of UB has a familiar structure. There is a Vice-Chancellor, who is an academic appointed by the Council, which is the equivalent of what we in Ontario call the Board of Governors. There is also a Senate, elected by the professors. The University consists of faculties, and they in turn consist of departments. Each department is headed by a Head of Department, what we in Canada call a department chair. The HOD is considered an important person. He or she is not elected but named by the dean who heads the faculty. Our dean took that responsibility very seriously and consulted each member of the department before naming a new HOD. When our department needed a temporary HOD because ours had been seconded to the Vice-Chancellor's office, I was on medical leave in Canada. The dean wrote to me for my opinion before he made the temporary appointment.

Once appointed, the HOD has considerable authority. The secretaries would say the phrase "HOD" in a hushed voice. The HOD assigned the courses the professors had to teach, s/he decided how to spend the departmental budget and could hire and replace the two secretaries without consulting anyone else. This is not to say that we did not have departmental meetings. We did, about once a month, usually in the morning. The meeting would begin at 9:00 am, and at 10:30 there would be break for tea, sandwiches and cookies. When the Head decided to save money by cutting out the "tea", there were many complaints and the tea reappeared at the next meeting.

The problem of people wanting to hear themselves talk at great length was even worse than it is in Canada. There was one professor who always went over the minutes with a fine toothcomb and, of course, usually found something that needed to be corrected. The minutes were taken not by the department secretary but a junior faculty member who was assigned that chore for the entire academic year.

Although meetings were long, few issues were ever decided. I tried to introduce some discussion of curricular matters but ran into lots of excuses for postponing such decisions. The department was wedded to the curriculum as it was. And the HOD sometimes felt free to ignore what the department had decided. In 2011, after I had returned to Canada on medical leave, I wrote an email to the HOD for circulation to the department, an email in which I thanked my colleagues for their kindness and hospitality and acceptance of me, a foreigner. I got no feedback and eventually realized that the HOD must have chosen not to circulate my email. On another occasion, a young lecturer, one who did not have his PhD, managed to gain admission to an American university. He went there but did not last long. The first year of course work defeated him. This man was the exception that proved all the rules: he was nasty and unpleasant and apparently also cancelled many classes. Shortly after arriving in the US, he wrote an email to many of us in the department, complaining about how badly we had treated him. The email was written in rude language. The matter was discussed at a department meeting, and HOD was instructed to write the man and tell him that this was uncollegial behaviour. HOD told me later that day that he had no intention of doing any such thing.

The department did decide about hirings. Whenever there was a position to fill, the CVs of all the candidates would be summarized in a table and circulated. We then had the option of looking at the actual applications. There were usually a fair number of applications, but many of them were rejected out of hand. Many did not have PhDs or had dubious qualifications. Then there was a strange university-wide rule that the person being considered needed to have a first degree in the field which s/he would teach. I found this absolutely ridiculous because many of us change fields as we go along, but this rule was used to weed out many people, such as Nigerians, who were considered otherwise undesirable. Because candidates were scattered all over the world, there were no interviews, not even by phone. Yet the process produced a reasonably good pool of colleagues, including me, of course. The problem cases were usually locals who had been hired some time ago, ran businesses on the side, and showed no interest in advancing beyond their MAs.

The University had a generous and sensible process for helping local lecturers with MAs obtain their PhDs. If the person gained admission to a PhD program, the University paid him or her a full salary for the first year and a partial salary for the following two years. With some scholarship money and/or research or teaching assistantships, this enabled a number of intelligent and hardworking colleagues to obtain PhDs, usually in Australia or the UK. In this way, the department developed a core of solid faculty with good qualifications.

There was one hiring process that particularly interested me. The former commander-in-chief of the Botswana Defence Force applied for a teaching position when he retired from the military. He was duly hired because of his experience, rather than his qualifications. The following year he departed midterm because a South African university had made him an attractive offer. He left his remaining classes untaught and left it to his colleagues, such as me, to correct papers that his students submitted.

When his work in South Africa was over, this former military officer once again applied to UB. He had good connections to our department. One of our colleagues had a link to the military and another was a former military officer. Besides, the man's former rank still impressed a number of colleagues. I argued strongly against hiring him again, but hired he was. A year later he announced that he was suffering from incurable glaucoma and that he would have to leave his position. I was very sympathetic at first and tried to help him find a clinic in India that specialized in the treatment of glaucoma.

Officer X duly left UB, only to resurface in the US where he was attached to a research institute, presumably on the basis of his former position with the BDF. He is now Botswana's High Commissioner to Nigeria. It would appear that the story about the incurable glaucoma was a ruse.

One of the problems that the department faced whenever it wanted to hire someone from outside Botswana was that the candidate had to obtain a work permit from the Ministry of Labour. Though there were provisions that allowed a professor to work on a temporary permit until the work permit was approved, this procedure did constitute an obstacle. As I mentioned earlier, the University employed a person who did nothing except handle these applications for faculty. She was very competent and had built up a good working relationship with the relevant officials in the Ministry.

About halfway through my time in Botswana, the government announced that it was cancelling all work permits for UB faculty. We would all have to reapply under slightly more stringent conditions. The human resources department invited all foreign faculty to a meeting for the purpose of explaining the new policy. Over one hundred persons attended. A university official and a government official explained the new policy. Everyone was puzzled as to what could be behind this move. In reply to a question, the university official said, "We want to keep *most* of you." This caused the room to break out in laughter, but the sense that either the government or the University no longer wanted some of us around was palpable.

Everyone I knew had their permits renewed, but we never did find out what was behind this move. Of all the rumours that abounded, the one that I found most credible was that the government was afraid of admitting Muslim fundamentalists from West African countries such as Nigeria. At the time I did not take this very seriously, but recent events in Nigeria (Boko Haram) demonstrate that the govern-ment would not have been so wrong to have such suspicions.

One task of UB department meetings that has no equivalent in Canada is known by the quaint term of *moderation*. Moderation has two parts. Before the final exams, all the exams had to be approved by the entire department. We considered each exam individually, a process that could take up to three to four hours. I kept myself awake and amused by picking apart everyone else's exams, finding fault with the English or the punctuation. This probably did not endear me to my colleagues, but they tolerated my input, for the most part, with good nature.

The second part of moderation resembles what some departments in Canada call grade meetings. We reviewed the final grades from every course taught in the department and looked for classes where the class average was much below or much above the average. Once or twice we forced junior faculty to go back over their grades and lower them. In Botswana as in Canada, professors who are not so sure of the quality of their teaching sometimes resort to generous grading to prevent students from complaining.

One term I had a small class of just three students in a graduate course with the cute title of Politics of the North. In North America we would call such a course Comparative Politics of Developed Countries. I gave all three students a B+. All were mature women students, and though they were not equally good, that is just how the grades worked out after I marked all the essays and the exam. One of the professors in the department had the nerve to comment that because these were mature women, perhaps not so different from me, I had identified with them and given them good grades. I was furious and refused to lower any of the grades, and the department allowed them to stand.

There were occasional departmental research seminars where visitors to Gaborone or members of the faculty presented their research. These were not that well attended. In addition, every MA student who wanted to write a thesis rather than just a major research paper had to present his/her proposal to the department for critical analysis. This was a useful exercise and was usually well attended.

It is a well-known fact that university administrators in Canada as in Botswana will do almost anything for money and the glory that comes with it, not so much for themselves but for their institutions and pet projects. Now Botswana does not have a military college. Indeed, when Botswana became independent, the first president hoped that it would not even need armed forces. However, when the racist Ian Smith regime across the border in Rhodesia (now Zimbabwe) started chasing its opponents into Botswana and the apartheid government in South Africa bombed houses in Gaborone where it believed refugees from apartheid might be living, killing twelve Batswana in the process, the Botswana government changed its mind. It created an army/air force, the Botswana Defence Force or BDF, which by now has grown to 10 000 personnel (mostly men, though some women have been added in recent years). The BDF is generously funded and has participated in a number of African peacekeeping missions. The current president is a former commander of the BDF who has brought a number of his old colleagues into the civil service. Happily, the army plays no obvious role in politics.

Some years ago, the University and the BDF began a partnership in which professors would teach courses to officers and receive a stipend in addition to their regular salaries. By 2012 the process had changed. Instead of having individual professors teach for the military, the BDF signed an agreement with the University whereby professors would teach for the military as part of their regular workload. In return, UB received a generous payment.

In January 2012 I was assigned to teach a graduate course on Foreign Policy Analysis at a military school somewhere in the outer suburbs of Gaborone. I hated the thought of teaching for the military, which I thought to be a particular odious bureaucracy wherever they are found. I tried to get out of this task by pointing out that I did not have a car and that a taxi both ways would cost more than the University would be willing to pay. There was a solution. The military had cars and drivers who did not have all that much to do. A military driver would pick me up at UB and drive me home after class.

My class was scheduled for 1:00 pm. I was expected to eat with senior officers at the complex and then teach my class. The food was dreadful, and the company was not much better; the food consisted of only meat and rice. Real men don't eat vegetables. The officers spoke in English so that I could understand, but the conversation was about routine matters and not very interesting. The commander of the school was particularly annoying. He told one story, which he considered to be a joke, over and over. It was apparently a true story about a married woman who went to study at the university in nearby Swaziland. Two years later, she came back pregnant. The village council met to decide whether the husband was obligated to take his wife back. He agreed to take her back, but only on condition that when the child was born, his or her name would be Moswazi, which means Swazi person. That was it. That was supposed to be the joke.

The officer students were a pleasant surprise. All had degrees, since this was a graduate course, but only two of the eight had degrees in the social sciences. The others were engineers. It was not easy to teach them at an appropriate level, but they tried so hard and did all their work on time. And they treated me with great respect, bringing me bottles of water, since the air conditioning in the classroom did not work well, and carrying my briefcase to the car. Everything had to be right on time. When it was time for the tea break, the class captain would point that out to me. These soldier-students had a heavy workload, as they were expected to participate in military exercises as well as carry a full course load. And many of them also had families.

Sometimes they had to stay up until three or four in the morning to get the course work done; as a result, some of them fell asleep in class. But I did not mention this to any of their commanders, because I had been told they could be punished for falling asleep in class.

They all worked hard; all eight of them attended every class and later they gave me the best teaching evaluations I have ever had. And they all passed with good grades. One of them is still in touch with me via the occasional email.

The next term the military gave me a larger undergraduate class to teach. It had 28 students, and the classes were no longer held on the suburban site but rather in a public-service college within walking distance of my house. With so many students, some of them did occasionally get sick and miss a class. But they were still a pretty nice bunch. There was a tea break during which the military supplied little sandwiches. These young men ate up every scrap of food, but they made sure that I had some before it all disappeared. And they all passed. I am still in touch with one of them, an officer who was once sent to Canada to learn French, in case the BDF was ever asked to do peacekeeping in a francophone African country.

I enjoyed my military students and have lost some of my prejudice against that particular bureaucracy.

At UB, all full professors university-wide were expected to give an "inaugural lecture" in which they presented an example of their research to the university community. This event was held in a large hall in the Continuing Education building and the Vice-Chancellor was expected to be in attendance. When I gave mine, on South African foreign policy, there was a good turnout, but the Vice-Chancellor sent the Dean of Education to replace him. I had to wear a big heavy University of Botswana gown and I had a student assistant turn the pages as I spoke. The lecture was always followed by a meal with wine — perhaps that is one reason attendance was so good. I was given a number of invitation cards to distribute as I liked. I gave one to Syntax, who was after all a university employee. He consulted with his friends but decided that it was not his place to attend. The meal after my lecture was particularly awful. I think it was the leftover lunch from that day.

Syntax's choosing not to attend my inaugural lecture was one of the few examples of class distinction that I noticed at UB. The faculty, support staff and cleaners — but not the undergraduate students — all bought lunch from the same cafeterias, though the cleaning staff did not usually stay in the cafeteria to eat. They took their food to the little broom-closet-like offices in each building that they occupied. One day, when I was in the library after lunch, I came across a group of cleaning ladies sitting on the floor between the shelves in the geography section, looking at pictures of various places in the world.

As in Canada, each faculty held a faculty council once a month, which we were all expected to attend. If a faculty member skipped more than three meetings in a row, s/he would be sent a reprimand from the Dean's office. Attendance was ascertained by a list which everyone had to sign as it circulated. Many people left after they had signed the list.

Faculty Council meetings were deadly dull, much more so than department meetings. There were reports from the senior administration on various matters that we could not do anything about anyway. Once there was a report about student participation in university affairs, but since there was no such participation that struck me as quite pointless.

One example of the pointlessness of the meetings at any level occurred during my second year at UB. The Senate and the Council had, after much discussion, decided to reorganize the University. The departments of statistics and population studies were to be transferred to the sciences, where the mathematics department was already housed. The department of economics was to go to the business school, and psychology would go to the new faculty of health sciences. That would have left the faculty of social sciences with just four departments, political science, sociology, social work and law. The dean, who had studied in Canada, said that this if this were Thanksgiving, the social science faculty was the turkey.

Before the process of transferring the departments to their new faculties was completed, a new Vice-Chancellor took office. With a stroke of his pen he cancelled the entire process, and the faculties stayed as they were. So much for collegial decision-making. In Canadian universities we pretend to have collegial decision-making, but in the end the big guys and gals get their way. At least at UB we knew what we were facing.

During the faculty council meetings, I at first chose to sit at the back and do some of my own work. I did not usually leave after signing the list because I found that to be unethical behaviour. Eventually I learned that scanning the agenda before the meeting might produce a few topics on which I could make some contributions. Hearing myself talk made the meetings a bit more interesting.

During my last term at UB, the social sciences had a great debate about access to the washrooms. The social science building was equipped with six large, clean and bright washrooms, one for each gender on each of the three floors. It was taken for granted that the students would steal whatever could be removed, even though I saw little evidence to support this assumption. As the result the liquid soap dispensers were always empty. Soap was dispensed from old plastic bottles placed on the side of each sink. I tried to point out that it was easier to steal soap from portable bottles than it was to steal it from dispensers underneath the sinks, but no one else seemed to share that logic.

Toilet paper was issued at the rate of one roll a week to each employee, and we needed to carry it with us when we went to use the washroom. Most people kept the toilet paper on their desk in full view. That is just how it was. The secretaries complained that they were given only one roll for the two of them, and they had to share that with visitors. I, on the other hand, did not need my full supply and took the leftover home when a new roll was issued.

Of the washrooms in the building, the ones on the second and third floors were supposed to be reserved for faculty and staff, and the ones on the first floor were for students. The students of course did not observe these distinctions. If they had a class on the second floor, they would use the washrooms there. For some reason this upset some of my colleagues, including the Dean. They wanted the students confined to their washrooms on the first floor.

Finally the Dean found a solution. The washrooms on the second and third floors would be equipped with electronic locks, and all the employees would be given tags that could fit onto a key chain. We could wave that tag over the lock and the washroom would open. In turn, the new locked washrooms were to be supplied with toilet paper, on the assumption that faculty and staff surely would not stoop to stealing the rolls.

At the Faculty Council, I did my best to oppose this notion, accusing my colleagues of being elitist and not treating their students with appropriate dignity. There were other solutions, I said, such as large industrial-size rolls of toilet paper or dispensers that dispensed one piece of paper at a time, but I had little support. The colleagues from my department kept silent, not wanting to oppose me, but the staff of Indian origin, of which there were quite a few in Population Studies and Statistics, favoured the new locked washrooms.

It did not take long for the locks to be installed and for the toilet paper rolls to disappear from the desks of my colleagues. Soap was still in short supply — I had long before resorted to keeping a small soap dish in my office — and by the afternoon, toilet paper was also scarce. I don't know if this was because of theft or because the supply was inadequate. But the new locks worked quite well. They did not malfunction while I was there, and the same electronic key worked for both the men's and women's washrooms, so that if we had a visitor, we could lend her or him our key.

The provision of washrooms around the University was very uneven. The library had washrooms that were open and accessible, as did the cafeteria buildings and any other academic buildings that I visited. They were all of the bring-your-own-toilet-paper variety. However, in the administration building, where the finance and human resources departments and the vice-chancellor's office were located, the washrooms were always supplied with both toilet paper and soap. And the washrooms were clean everywhere; plugged toilets and sinks were quickly attended to. The only problem was that in some buildings, notably our social science building, the water supply sometimes dried up, usually because workers on one of the new buildings had to disconnect it to make some new connections or because they broke a pipe by accident. That forced us to use the toilets in the library, a five-minute walk away. There the water almost always worked.

Final Comments

With these washroom stories I end my account of life in Botswana and UB. I miss the University. If I could, I would go back in a flash. When I returned to Gaborone for a visit in 2014, some students who were still there came up to me and with great delight shouted, "You have come back!" Most of my students and colleagues treated me with much genuine affection and respect. But I have family in Canada, and further, in Botswana I could not participate in politics (my passion) because I was not a citizen. All good things do often come to an end. But hardly a day passes without pleasant memories of my life at the University of Botswana.

AN INTRODUCTION TO BOTSWANA:
IF YOU WANT TO KNOW MORE

You could do worse than to start with Martin Meredith, *Diamonds, Gold and War. The British, the Boers and the Making of South Africa.* (New York: Public Affairs, 2007). This is a wonderfully readable book about the origins of the Boer War, the origins of apartheid, the life of Cecil Rhodes and also the birth of the national consciousness of the Tswana people.

Next I would read a short biography, *Little Giant of Bechuanaland: a biography of William Charles Willoughby, Missionary and Scholar* (by John Rutherford. Gaborone: Mmegi, 2009). Willoughby was a British missionary to the Bangwato tribe of central Bechuanaland in the 1890s, and more importantly was an associate of Khama the Great, the chief whose policies did most to secure eventual independence.

The books by Rutherford and Meredith are good background reading for the next book: Neil Parsons, *King Khama, Emperor Joe and the Great White Queen: Victorian Britain through African Eyes* (University of Chicago Press, 1998), which is the story of how Willoughby and three Tswana chiefs travelled to England to save their country from Cecil Rhodes's imperial ambitions. This is a long detailed book, only for the seriously interested.

If you want a glimpse of what village life was like at the time of independence, before diamond wealth infused Botswana, read Unity Dow, *Juggling Truths* (Spinifex Press, 2004), which is supposed to be fiction, but which is really her memoir of life as a schoolgirl.

For a look at village life a bit later, there is Bessie Head, *When Rain Clouds Gather* (Reissued by Macmillan, 2008). This is a novel set in the days of apartheid. Bessie Head, now deceased, is Botswana's national author so to speak, who was once a refugee from apartheid in South Africa. I think that Unity Dow, a former judge and now a politician, is a better writer.

Dow's best book is *The Screaming of the Innocent* (Spinifex Press, 2002), a thriller of a novel, which catches the flavour of life on the cusp between modernity and tradition, and is a darn good read besides.

For a glimpse of life in contemporary Botswana, you could try *Saturday is for Funerals* by Unity Dow and Max Essex (Cambridge: Harvard University Press, 2011), a real-life account of the ravages of HIV/AIDS.

There is, sad to say, no formal history of Botswana except one out-of-date high school text. That job remains to be done. Anyone interested?

And for fun and escapism, there are the fifteen books of the No. 1 Ladies Detective series, all written by Alexander McCall Smith. They provide insights into the life of a middle-class family, and they are all good fun to read. Read the first one, for context. After that, of the fourteen I have read, *The Tears of the Giraffe* and *The Kalahari Typing School for Men* are my personal favourites.

Finally, I have created a Facebook page for my own book. Here I offer all of the photos in colour, and I also hope to interact with you, my readers. Please see https://www.facebook.com/Grandmasgonetoafrica and join the discussion.

Made in the USA
Charleston, SC
18 April 2016